CW00695460

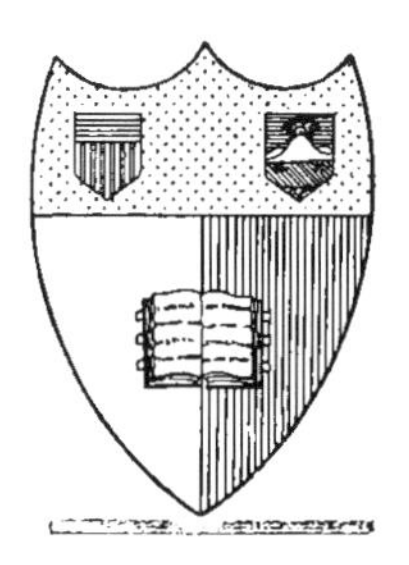

HOME USE RULES

All Books subject to recall

All borrowers must register in the library to borrow books for home use.

All books must be returned at end of college year for inspection and repairs.

Limited books must be returned within the four week limit and not renewed.

Students must return all books before leaving town. Officers should arrange for the return of books wanted during their absence from town.

Volumes of periodicals and of pamphlets are held in the library as much as possible. For special purposes they are given out for a limited time.

Borrowers should not use their library privileges for the benefit of other persons.

Books of special value and gift books, when the giver wishes it, are not allowed to circulate.

Readers are asked to report all cases of books marked or mutilated.

Do not deface books by marks and writing.

THE ANNALS

OF

A LITTLE LONDON HOUSE

'East or West.—Hame's Best.'

Our Square & Circle

OR THE

ANNALS OF A LITTLE LONDON HOUSE

BY

JACK EASEL

sometime PUNCH'S '*Roving Correspondent*

New York

MACMILLAN AND CO.

1895

CONTENTS

OUR SQUARE AND CIRCLE

CHAPTER I

'TERRA-COTTAGE'

SHORTLY after I had entered on possession of my house in Dexter Square, Bayswater, I dined with my old friend Banterfield, and described to him with no small satisfaction the various attractions and conveniences of that abode. His congratulations were hearty, but they would have pleased me more if he had been able to recall the exact locality of the residence, which he persisted in regarding as very remote. It was in vain I pointed out to him that it was within three minutes' walk of Kensington Gardens, exactly midway between two well-known lines of omnibus routes, not far from a Metropolitan Railway station, and very handy to Eastbourne Avenue, where Blackwood's great emporium daily attracts a thousand customers. The provoking wretch would have it that I had gone to live in some suburban spot extremely difficult of access, and when wishing me good-bye at his own door at 11 P.M., he expressed a hope that I should find my way home on such a dark night, in case the street gas lamps had not yet been extended to Dexter Square. Gas lamps indeed! Why the Square has been built for thirty years at least, and is as well lighted as any part of London. But Banterfield would always have his joke, and to do him justice he has since confessed, after inspecting the house, that my choice was a good one.

Dexter Square is laid out on an ingenious plan. The fronts of the houses are approached from a street, and the back windows look into the Square garden, which you may enter direct from the dining-room without crossing a road. When the trees are in full leaf you can scarcely see the opposite houses through the foliage of plane-trees or limes; the turf is kept in order; the gravel paths are neatly rolled; the flower beds are gay with stocks, tiger-lilies, marigolds, lilac and laburnum, geraniums, hyacinths, crocuses and daffodils—a pleasant sight in the midst of cloud-capped, sooty London, as we sit at breakfast on a summer morning. Moreover, each house has a little *parterre* of its own, railed off by balustrading and a wicket from the public garden, and affording a cool retreat in the dog-days for those who like an after-dinner cigar and cup of coffee. The turf outside forms a favourite promenade for the young people in twilight, and, without being unduly inquisitive, I have become aware that it is occasionally used as a flirtation ground by the sons and daughters of our neighbours, who meet here in friendly intercourse, and perhaps with less restraint than in the drawing-rooms of Dexter Square, though prudent *materfamilias* may be keeping a watchful eye upon them over her novel or needlework on the balcony overhead.

It was in this convenient resort, I am told, that young FitzSpooner first made known his deep attachment to pretty Kate Papillon, and here, too, that Captain Shyleigh (home on sick-leave from India) summoned up courage to propose to the second Miss Chattermore, before rejoining his regiment at Bombay. Many other matches, I have reason to believe, have been made up in our Square garden, and since such incidents must occur, and there comes a time in every man's life when he has to choose a partner, I confess that I think an *al fresco* declaration in the cool of the evening is more likely to be based on a discreet and honest judgment, than if he plunged into an engagement after whirling round a heated ball-room with the object of his affections, or settled his fate during a cricket-match at Lord's, under the transient influence of Heidsieck Monopole.

The entrance to our house is, as I have said, from

a street which, as it lies midway between and parallel to two great thoroughfares, possesses the singular advantage of being a short cut to nowhere, and is therefore comparatively quiet even in the height of the season. The ceaseless roar of traffic and noise of wheels which belong to more fashionable neighbourhoods are unknown here, and though the inhabitants of Dexter Square are within easy access of smart shops, cab ranks, and all the conveniences of habitable London, and can be in the midst of life and bustle by walking a few dozen yards, when they re-enter their own demesne it is as quiet and secluded a spot as one could hope to find in the centre of a busy capital, and after dusk the silence which reigns around, so beneficent and soothing to the worried nerves of a hard-worked man, is that of a rural retreat.

In the early morning hours certainly the itinerant chair-mender and the peripatetic coal merchant will occasionally make their voices heard, but they only prevent one from sleeping too long, and just as we are informed on an eminent authority that 'the uses of adversity' are sweet, so it may be inferred that these lugubrious cries are not without a certain advantage in counteracting matutinal laziness.

And then to think of the advantage of living in a house with a large open space, and free current of air circulating as sailors would say, fore and aft. No dismal yards, no back settlements, no dingy walls or dirty stables to look out upon, but a street of smart-looking, cheerful houses on one side, with green turf and green trees on the other! When I remember some of the dull and dusty tenements of a corresponding size which cost the occupiers 300*l.* or 400*l.* a year in a fashionable neighbourhood, when I recollect the mingled odours of mews and dust-cart which prevail in some of the smaller thoroughfares of Mayfair, I feel thankful that my social ambition has not taken a residential form, and that I am able to live for half the rent above mentioned in a light, well-ventilated home.

As to the external appearance of our abode, there is nothing in an architectural sense to boast of. It was built long before the so-called 'Queen Anne revival began. Consequently it possesses no picturesque details to delight the eye—no mullioned windows or dainty casements, no canopied porch or moulded niches, no pretty string courses or tall chimney-shafts, no steep roofs or pedimental dormers, no carved panels or quaintly fashioned rain-pipes. It is a mere substantial-looking builder's house, with a few balconies front and back, and a façade which, though eminently respectable, can hardly be called interesting. Such conventional features as it includes—pilasters, cornices, window dressings, and a festooned frieze—are, it must be confessed, executed in cement, and this being so, the only chance of concealing their mediocrity was to cover them with paint in two shades of the same colour, for the choice of which I am responsible.

Now, colour is a matter of taste, which in the case of house-painting shows itself in infinite varieties. Some of my neighbours seem to have a fancy for pea-green, some for sky-blue. Others incline to chocolate-brown, which certainly does not show the London soot, but, on the other hand, it affords unusual temptations to the passing street boy, who, thanks to the School Board, has learnt to write, and goes about with a fine lump of white chalk in his pocket. So, after various experiments, we decided on two shades of terra-cotta, the lighter shade for the walls and the darker for pilasters, cornices, &c. This ‘ chromatic scheme ’ (as the art critics have it) was generally pronounced a success by our friends and neighbours, and though Banterfield, when asked what he thought of it, made some frivolous comparison to anchovy paste, it must be remembered that he is a Philistine, utterly ignorant of æsthetics, and so we don’t mind *his* remarks at all. He calls our house *Terra-cottage*.

We painted our railings a dull red, like the colour of an old Greek vase, and used the same tint for our front door. In the centre of the latter, just within easy reach of the postman’s arm, is affixed an ancient and quaintly shaped iron knocker, which I found on a chalet in Switzerland. We were coming down from the Rieder-Alp, I remember, one blazing hot afternoon in September. The rustic owner stood at his portal smoking a pipe, and was greatly amused at the curiosity with which I examined his knocker. After a little preliminary parley he offered to sell it for five francs, and in a few minutes I was trudging off with my bargain. We were all delighted to get it, except my wife's maid, who viewed the acquisition with a smile of scorn. 'Law bless me, m'am,' said the artless creature, 'master's surely never going to carry back that old rubbish to London!' But he did though, and there it hangs on my door, which is frequently struck with it. So by the way are many of our afternoon callers.

Owing to the peculiar plan of our house (and here I may say in a parenthesis that your builders' architect is often a person with remarkable views on the subject of planning) the entrance hall is limited in size. At a guess it measures about ten feet by eight, so that there is just space enough for a hall table and chair besides the umbrella and hat stand. But, by an ingenious disposition of those indispensable articles of furniture, there is still room enough left for two persons to pass each other without jostling. Indeed, I have known it to hold three, but this is to be avoided if possible, especially when General O'Currie, who weighs about fifteen stone, is struggling into his fur-lined overcoat, and his arms are flying about like the sails of a windmill.

I had the cement floor replaced by one of encaustic tiles of a size proportionate to so small an area. I was reluctantly obliged to reject the first design submitted to me by Messrs. Hercules, Pompey & Co., not because I did not like it, for it was unimpeachable in taste, but because I found that the available floor space would have been all occupied by border. The same restrictions as to scale compel me to confess that the reindeer's antlers hung over the oak hall table (though as near the ceiling as possible) are somewhat bulky for their position. But as they were a present from Cousin Bridget, who has shared our home for the last ten years, and who brought them all the way from the North Cape, I was bound to find a place for them, and they certainly add dignity to the entrance.

I found room on the walls for some prints and engravings, including Macbeth's fine etching from Titian's 'Bacchus and Ariadne.

What an ineffable charm there is in that famous picture! Although the spirit of the Renaissance is manifest in every line of the composition, it is unencumbered by pseudo-classicism or antiquarian pedantry. The youthful vine-crowned lover leaping from his chariot with his peach-coloured mantle fluttering in the breeze, is an active yeoman rather than a god. The nymphs and fauns who follow dancing in his train are peasant girls and rustics. Even the deserted princess herself is a mere buxom lass, undistinguished by any ideal beauty of limb or feature. But what a sense of jocund action and vigorous humanity pervades the group! There is life and motion in every figure. The supple forms seem to spring or glide over the turf beneath the shade of those tall beech trees. You may almost hear the jubilant shouts of the sylvan throng and listen to the merry jingle of their music as the procession wends its way towards the shore. See, yonder is Silenus, fuddled as usual, and bestriding his ass, with a faithful friend by his side to support him. High up in the heavens above Ariadne's head we see the constellation of the golden crown—the bridal gift of her new lover, and far away in the distance, calmly sailing over the blue Ægean Sea, is the vessel which bears away the faithless Theseus and his crew.

It is interesting to pass from this work, executed in the early part of the sixteenth century, to the modern treatment of a similar subject painted at the close of the nineteenth. In the same tiny entrance hall hangs an engraving from Alma Tadema's picture of 'The Vintage Festival.' Here we have another procession of a Bacchanalian character, but instead of wildly dancing in the chequered shade, it passes with measured steps along a colonnade of the Corinthian order, festooned with garlands, surrounding the *atrium* of a Roman temple. At its head is a young woman draped in a white tunic, her fair hair bound up with grape bunches and vine leaves. In her hand she bears a burning torch, and as she walks along with graceful dignity she looks back with an approving smile towards the *tibicinæ* who follow at a respectful distance. We can see that they are beautiful, though their features are half masked by the ugly apparatus which binds the flageolets to their heads. To them succeed two laughing tambour players, who toss up their jingling instruments with gleeful action. After them come two solemn, bearded male priests bearing *amphoræ*, filled, let us say, with choice Falernian, and behind them a damsel, carrying a basket of grapes and a drinking vessel, brings up the rear.

In the foreground is a tripod altar of bronze raised upon a marble pedestal enriched with bas-relief. A little towards the left is a huge earthenware vase—a *dolium* I think the scholars call it—and on the right lies a thyrsus just laid aside. In the middle distance a merry crowd, dancing or playing on musical instruments, fills the hypæthral court, and on a bench in the corridor sits a prætor, or some person of importance, who gazes from afar with a gesture of rapt admiration at the fair priestess.

These two prints are both favourites of mine, but though they hang near each other, and the subjects are somewhat similar, it is difficult, almost impossible, to compare them. Each is admirable in its way, and there is a certain affinity of object in the two painters' aims. But how differently their taste, their quality of work, their mode of treatment! You might as well try to draw a parallel between Dryden's Ovid and Swinburne's 'Atalanta,' between an Elizabethan representation of 'King Lear' and Mr. Irving's Shakesperian revivals, between the performance of a Greek chorus and one of Wagner's operas. Three centuries separate Alma Tadema from Titian. Before the great Venetian's picture we stand enthralled by the charm of colour, the facile distribution of light and shade, the amazing dexterity of composition, the vigour of his brush, the daring departure from archaic precedent, and the human interest which the painter gives to a mere romantic myth.

The modern Royal Academician approaches his subject more diffidently perhaps, but with a consummate sense of beauty, with a just appreciation of truth, with a technical skill which has rarely been surpassed, and with the advantage of antiquarian knowledge and research of which his predecessor never dreamed.

Alma Tadema's figures, let us confess it, are more gracefully proportioned than those on Titian's canvas; they are far more appropriately draped; the accessories assume correcter forms. There is an air of realism about the scene. The actual life of ancient Rome is brought before us as though by a clever photographer. In Titian's design we only see a highly poetical rendering of a scene in Naxos.

Between these two phases of art there is a wide span. But we eclectics of the Victorian age admire everything in turn: Egyptian sphinxes, Nineveh bulls, Greek bas-reliefs, Roman mosaics, Michel Angelo and Vanucci, Botticelli and Burne-Jones, Leonardo da Vinci and Landseer. In the whirligig of time we adopt classic, mediæval, and Queen Anne architecture. So, too, we read indiscriminately Chaucer and Rudyard Kipling, Milton and Lewis Morris, Ben Jonson and Mr. Gilbert. Truly we are omnivorous in matters of taste, whether structural, pictorial, or literary.

That a porch of such modest size as that which forms the entrance to our house should contain any furniture at all is a wonder. But you must have a place to hang up your hats and stow away your umbrellas on the threshold of every Christian homestead, or where are you? Again, the page-boy, who comes with three-cornered notes from our good neighbour Miss Medlicott asking for the loan of my Post

Office Directory, or begging my wife to send her that *too delicious* recipe for curried lobster—this silver-buttoned emissary, I say, must be provided with a seat while he waits for an answer, and so a hall chair becomes indispensable. Respecting these two useful articles I have little to say beyond the expression of an earnest wish that lady callers would fold up their umbrellas and parasols before depositing them in the stand, for, what with the limited accommodation at our disposal and the fact of my being near-sighted, I have on more than one occasion put the ferrule of my favourite walking stick straight through the elegant twill silk covering of a fashionable sunshade or *en-tout-cas* left sprawling open inside the rail, and as a confession of these misadventures would involve an outlay of at least twelve shillings and sixpence a time, I cannot afford to be ingenuous on such occasions, and as a necessary result am conscience-smitten when I see my visitors to the door.

But in my hall table I take an honest pride. It is of solid oak, and designed by myself at a time when the so-called 'art-furniture' was unknown, with mouldings and incised carved work of a sixteenth-century pattern, and having been well rubbed with oil for the last twenty years has acquired a rich dark colour so that it is frequently taken for an 'antique.' It has a couple of shelves for the display of china, and a couple of drawers, one handy for gloves (it is astonishing how soon a dozen pairs accumulate), and the other in which my wife hoards a vast store of visiting cards left by her friends and acquaintances. Of the latter I know many by name and some by sight. But when I try to identify them with their respective visiting cards, I get, as Americans say, a little 'mixed.' For instance, when walking the other day in Kensington Gardens we met a very charming woman, who greeted my wife most affectionately, but I had not the wildest notion what her name was. I felt that I ought to inquire after her husband, but I hesitated, for she might be unmarried or a widow. It would have been only civil to express a hope that the children were well—but, good heavens! perhaps she had no family. We took leave of her, and it was only when she was walking away that I found that we had been talking to the Lady Wilhelmina Stubbs, whom we had met at dinner a month ago. On another occasion a man button-holed me at the Club, and offered to send my wife a couple of stalls for a concert if I would drop him a line to say whether she would go. I thanked him gratefully, promised that I would write by that evening's post, but who or what he was I no more knew than the man in the moon. The situation grew extremely embarrassing, but I was saved by a stratagem. I confessed that I had forgotten the number of the street in which he lived, and on this plea I asked him for his card. He gave it, thinking me no doubt a duffer, but even that was better than having to tell the truth.

How is any man, occupied with his daily work, to remember everyone whom he meets accidentally in London society? One's acquaintance goes on increasing like a snowball. We dine out a great deal —I fear far more often than is good for me. Well, say I take the bewitching Mrs. Smyth-Smythe down to dinner. Ten to one Mrs. Smyth-Smythe expresses a wish to know my wife. On the other hand, my wife herself sits next the Hon. Gwythyr Ap-Jones whose monograph on the disintegration of Stonehenge created such a *furore* in antiquarian circles last season. Personally I never heard of his book, but my wife vows I am much interested in the subject, and thus the two gentlemen are brought together in the drawing-room. The following week my door-knocker thunders twice distinctly under the influence of fresh hands. Cards are exchanged—one for each of the ladies and two apiece for the gentlemen, because, I suppose, they are printed on a smaller scale—with a net result that two new families are added to our visiting list.

By-and-by we shall dine with the Smyth-Smythes, and the Ap-Joneses will be bidden to our humble board. At each house there will be fresh introductions, and so it goes on *ad infinitum*. It is the women who manage these things—bless their effusive little hearts!—on a sort of 'more the merrier' principle, and so it comes to pass that the drawer of my hall table gradually overflows with pasteboard.

Passing through the glazed door which separates our hall from the adjoining passage, visitors find themselves opposite to a huge mirror ingeniously let into a recess of the wall. This contrivance, besides affording young ladies an excellent opportunity for reflection, has the effect of widening the corridor and creating the impression—transient, indeed, but first impressions are important—of a double staircase, which in a tenement of only twenty feet frontage is almost phenomenal. It is true that guests ascending to the drawing-room see duplicates of themselves engaged in the same pursuit. But this gives an air of symmetry to the affair which in a well-balanced mind must be a source of satisfaction.

And this reminds me of a curious incident which happened to me a few years ago. In a moment of weakness I had accepted an invitation to a fancy-dress ball at a friend's house—rather a rash act for a middle-aged man who has long given up dancing, and does not care to make a guy of himself in costume. I compromised the matter by appearing in levee-dress, to which, *elegantiæ gratiâ*, as the grammarians say, I added a magnificent white satin waistcoat, elaborately embroidered with coloured silk, after the fashion in vogue at Court half a century ago. Having done my duty by entering the ball-room, and having watched the young people capering about in every conceivable attire for nearly an hour, I strolled from the festive scene towards an ante-chamber, where, as I thought, a supplementary quadrille was going on. Just as I was passing under the rather dimly lighted archway which led from one room to another, I saw coming towards me a man with whom I believed I had a slight acquaintance. Not being quite sure whether he would recognise me, I stood still for a moment and observed that he did the same. He then looked at me, and as he did not speak I moved aside to let him pass. But, like many people when they run across each other in the street, he took a step in the same direction as myself and stood confronting me. I smiled and saw that he was equally amused. I then felt sure that he remembered me, and I held out my hand. He did the same with his, but it seemed to elude my grasp. Somewhat disconcerted I was going to turn aside, when he again stood in my way. A moment and I stumbled against a mirror! I had actually mistaken myself for somebody else. It was a most stupid thing to do—but I could only apologise to myself and walk away.

And this reminds me that I am digressing in another sense.

The ground floor passage in my house is narrow, I admit, but it is far wider than that in the residence of my old friend Sir Rackstraw Stableton, Bart., who lives half way down a mews in Mayfair, and is visited by some of the smartest people in London. In our own little domicile there is, at least, plenty of light from the staircase window, and if the dining-room door is open, you look right through the windows in that apartment on to the garden, giving the uninitiated visitor a transient impression that the house stands in its own grounds. Indeed, when I regard the vista myself at the close of a quiet day, I feel a sort of content akin to that which, after a general survey of his estate, must be experienced by a landed proprietor.

CHAPTER II

OUR DINING-ROOM

If there is one part of the house more than another which I regard with tolerable satisfaction (and I am not referring to what used to be called 'the pleasures of the table') it is the dining-room. In respect to size a few more feet in length would certainly have added to its convenience. But it will hold a dozen guests comfortably—and what domestic feast was ever bettered by a larger number? It is not, however, on 'party nights,' when the room is glittering with plate, smart dresses, and gewgaws, that it looks its best. I am pleased with it in the quiet of a summer evening, when one can look round and think how far a little taste, a little patience, and a little money will go to enliven the four walls of a commonplace London house.

Perhaps my approval is partly due to the fact that most of the furniture in this room was designed expressly for myself. It dates from a period when the ordinary and material appearance of our homes was at the mercy of the upholsterer, and a terrible time it was. Young housekeepers of the present age who sit in picturesque chimney corners, sipping tea out of Oriental china, or lounge on 17th-century settles, in a parquetry-floored room filled with inlaid cabinets, Cromwell chairs, picturesque sideboards, hanging shelves and bookcases, can form no idea of the heavy and graceless objects with which an English house was filled some twenty years ago—the sprawling sofas, the gouty-legged dining tables, cut-glass chandeliers, lumbering ottomans, funereal buffets, horticultural carpets and zoological hearth-rugs. Heaven save us from a return to that phase of ugly conventionalism, of lifeless ornament, of dull propriety, and inartistic gloom!

Well, from this slough of despond I was rescued at an early period of my domestic career by the author of a little book which advocated a reform in such matters. Influenced thenceforth by his doctrines, and guided by his advice, I had most of my furniture made expressly for me, added to it from time to time, directed the paper-hanger, controlled the painter, supervised the carpet man, and made the interior of my house what I wanted it to be—rather picturesque.

At first, of course, the style of my furniture was the subject of severe chaff from my friends. My favourite sideboard, which has upper shelves filled with blue-and-white china, was compared to a kitchen dresser. My substantial oaken settle, in the proportions of which

I had endeavoured to combine modern comfort with the spirit of the fifteenth century, reminded my critics, as they kindly told me, of a second-class railway carriage. Some of them found fault with the height of my chimney-piece fender (although it is barely two feet from the floor and is an admirable safeguard from fire). Others complained of the cross-bars in front of my Cromwell chairs, though they are beautifully covered with green morocco and stamped in gilt on the back with the family crest—a *chevalet* proper, and the motto 'NULLA DIES SINE LINEA.' Some said my clock ticked too loudly—my beloved clock, a beautiful specimen of 17th-century brass-work, which I bought in Paris ten years ago for forty francs, and which has cost me at least that sum annually for repairs ever since. Others suggested that my corona lamp imparted an ecclesiastical character to the room and implied a partiality for ritualism. Perhaps the kindest and most judicious critics of all were those who approved of this or that detail in my scheme of decoration, but regretted that they were misplaced. For instance, I had devised a 'frieze' of stamped-leather panels for the walls, and formed a 'dado' of 'Lincrusta Walton.' Now Bob Carpington, who writes for 'The Æsthete,' to do him justice, admired both. He only hinted that the frieze should have been of 'Lincrusta Walton' and the dado of stamped leather. 'Of course it can't be helped now,' said that gifted connoisseur amiably, 'but there is no doubt *that* would have been the thing to do.'

Lord bless us! if we all listened to monitors who tell us what we *ought* to have done—generally the reverse of what we *have* done—what a miserable world this would be.

About myself personally I don't so much mind. People may say that I wear my beard too short, that I smoke too much, that I ought to rise earlier, that I am inclined to banter, that I am intolerant of long sermons, and what not. *Video meliora proboque.* But really when it comes to matters of taste, and in his own house too, if a man may not do as he likes, there is an end to the liberty of the subject. So I am not going to be put out of conceit with my little dining-room, which for its size, and considering it only forms part of a commonplace tenement, is, I venture to think, rather effective. I had the walls painted pale green to form a good background for pictures, of which I have a few, picked up from time to time, and all bargains, for I can't afford long prices.

There is a long horizontal battle-piece attributed to Campagnola, which evidently formed the front of an old Italian *cassone*. I bought it in Venice years ago and brought it away from the Manfrin Palace in a gondola. It is painted on panel, and represents a camp with a number of tents stretching away in rapid perspective towards a background of blue mountains. In the nearest tent sits a lordly personage watching a terrific but apparently bloodless skirmish between cavalry and infantry, which is going on outside. The warriors are clad in a sort of semi-classic costume, and for what I know it may be an incident in the second Punic War, but it is no use to bother one's head about chronology or propriety of costume in a picture of the 16th century. Some of the figures are queerly drawn, but they are full of life and action. The scheme of colour is excellent and the landscape very charming. It is what the dealers call a 'decorative' work, and after all what could be more suited for its purpose? You don't want a moral preached at you from your dining-room walls. You want something to brighten the house, and make you forget the gloom of London air.

Above this picture hangs a life-size portrait of Cosmo II., Grand Duke of Tuscany—a stolid-looking personage as depicted on this canvas (possibly by Sustermans); it is by no means an attractive painting, but it is inclosed in a pretty old frame, enriched with cinque-cento ornament in low relief, and it forms a good centre for the wall. Right and left of it are smaller portraits of Mary Queen of Scots, and the Princess Elizabeth (afterwards good Queen Bess), both charmingly attired in the picturesque dresses of the period. What beautiful brocades and embroidery! Would that our modern looms and workshops produced such now. But in those days robes and gowns were not made for a 'season,' to be thrown aside and called old-fashioned next year. Women's dress—and men's too, for that matter—was a work of art affording exercise for genuine taste, not the result of a milliner's freak. Oh ladies, ladies, if you would but recognise this fact, and try to infuse a little character and common-sense into your costumes, instead of adopting your milliners' notions of what is 'elegant' and 'novel,' what a reform you might effect in the art of dress, and how grateful the portrait painters—not to mention your lovers and husbands—would be for the change!

Pray don't suppose that I am advocating a return to the craze for what were known as 'æsthetic' garments, which prevailed in certain circles some years ago, when women draped themselves in sage-green bathing gowns with terra-cotta neckerchiefs, and hats which looked as if they had been bought from a theatrical costumier. I don't want your figures to look like woolsacks or scarecrows; I don't want your hair to be dressed like a fancy coloured mop; I don't want your mantle collars to conceal your throats, nor your sleeves to make you look high-shouldered. I should like you to wear clothes which are graceful and convenient, and to wear them because they are pretty to look at, deftly designed and harmonious in colour—*not* because they are either eccentric or the latest novelty from Paris. I abhor tight lacing, first, because it is, as any medical man will tell you, ruinous to health, and, secondly, because it makes the human waist cylindrical, like a ninepin, which Nature never intended. I hate high heels, because they torture the feet and destroy the poetry of motion. I dislike your V-shaped bodices cut down fore and aft, and leaving the arms naked, because they are both indelicate and ugly. I detest unduly long skirts because one is always treading on them. Your great-grandmothers in 1815 wore skirts six inches off the ground, and so narrow that they could not with any sense of decency get over a stile. That was absurd. You, on the contrary, let your gowns fall into trains of a yard and a half in length behind you, sweeping up dust from the pavement, or tripping up elderly gentlemen as they come down-stairs. That is absurder still.

Again, well-fitting gloves, which terminate just above the wrist, showing the shape of the hand, are right enough. But gloves with forty-eight buttons which run up to the shoulder are troublesome abominations. Away with them! Real taste does not regulate these matters, but pure caprice, and the best proof of this is that when by a rare stroke of luck a reasonable and becoming article of dress becomes fashionable, it is discarded in the course of a season or two. Not many years ago ladies' hats were very picturesque—I mean the oval broad-brimmed ones—not those of the detestable 'pork-pie' type. Where are they now? Banished in favour of a crownless trencher perched on the top of the head, and pinned there Heaven knows how. As for bonnets, they have been explained away altogether, and we get in their place a lump of milliner's trumpery, without form and void; while that useful and modest appendage, the veil, has degenerated into a net mask, fixed so tightly over the face that it turns the wearer's eyelids half inside out, when the lashes brush against it.

There are a few other pictures worth looking at in my dining-room. A group of saints centred by Madonna, supporting on her knees a beautiful Infant Christ, who raises His tiny hand to bless St. John the Baptist and St. Roch, while St. Joseph and St. James stand reverently in the rear:—a sober and graceful work by Bissolo, who caught something of Bellini's charm without rivalling his skill.

In the opposite corner hangs a somewhat similar composition by an unknown Venetian painter of the same period—not so well drawn but richer in colour, and enshrined in a pretty frame which I believe to be as old as the painting itself. This picture was the first 'Old Master' we ever dared to buy, and I remember feeling some scruples when I drew a cheque to pay for it in Venice, thinking that we ought not to have afforded what seemed in those days to us an extravagant price for the work.

On another wall there is a small equestrian portrait ascribed to Van der Meulen, representing a young and gentle-looking field marshal in a fine plumed hat, embroidered leathern doublet and jack-boots, mounted on a gaily caparisoned charger, prancing in a landscape by twilight.

On the other side of the sideboard a handsome boy of sixteen, clad in a plum-coloured coat and lace ruffle, looks out with a kindly but dignified smile from the canvas of Sir Godfrey Kneller. I know neither the name nor the history of this youth—whether he ever grew to man's estate, whether he married and, if so, whether he left any children. How many portraits there must be in the world over which the same obscurity hangs! A century or so before Kneller's time the artist would probably have inscribed his sitter's name in gold characters in a corner of the background. We may smile nowadays at this antiquated custom, but after all it was based on common-sense, and if it had always prevailed I think posterity would have been grateful.

Just below my 'Kneller' is a gilt frame about twelve inches square, with an inner flat composed of ivory plaques carved in low relief, and enclosing a circular panel on which is painted a St. Cecilia bearing a palm branch, with her organ emblem in the background. This little picture presents an enigma which I have never been able to solve. The ivory plaques are of earlier date than the painting. The painting itself is older than the gilt-wood mouldings by which it is enclosed. The frame is evidently not a modern one, and yet it differs both in design and character from any specimen I have ever seen of ancient handicraft. Here is a nice little riddle for the *cognoscenti*. The saint's face is pretty and delicately painted, with large upturned eyes, clusters of chestnut-brown hair, and lips parted as though in song. It is probably by an Italian painter, but of what age or school I cannot say. After all what does it matter? An old friend of mine used to say that he would undertake to form one of the most interesting collections in Europe if he could only select from every public picture gallery all the works labelled 'ignoto,' 'inconnu,' and 'unbekannt.' There are not so many as there used to be, for in our time the scientific critics have been at work, and their discoveries have deprived us to a great extent of the pleasures of speculation.

Fortunately, however, your learned *dilettante* of today is sure to be contradicted by the gifted connoisseur of to-morrow, and if the ultimate result of all this dogmatic guess-work should be to let future lovers of art once more indulge in their own tastes and fancies, no great harm will have been done, and the world will have learnt a lesson.

No one at present has ventured to question the authenticity of one picture in this room—a bust-length portrait of a man, by William Dobson (the English limner whose master was knighted by Charles I., and who himself was rescued from obscurity and befriended by Van Dyck). He is said with truth to have caught something of the style and manner of his great patron. Perhaps he learnt something of his extravagance too, for when, after the opulent Fleming's death, Dobson was appointed Court painter to his Majesty, he lived in good style and did not think of saving for his old age, which he passed, I fear, in poverty.

Moralists of that age, and of the present too, will no doubt cry fie upon the spendthrift, and it must be confessed that to live beyond your means is very reprehensible. But if a man of social habits, with a modest income and a large circle of friends, finds himself the object of frequent hospitality, he must either decline or return it. If in adopting the latter course poor Dobson tried to vie with his wealthier friends in the way of entertainment, he was foolish, but I fear that this species of folly is as frequent in the 19th as it was in the 17th century.

When shall we learn wisdom in such matters? A wealthy banker, let us say, invites me to dinner. His house, compared with my modest domicile, is a palace. It is fitted up and furnished with splendour. The table glitters with costly plate, is decorated with hot-house flowers, and loaded with every delicacy in and out of season. Wines of the choicest vintage are set before you: 'Heidsieck Monopole' and Château Lafite of 1875. The menu records the achievements of a French *chef*. You are served by half a dozen footmen resplendent in new livery. The banquet is elegant, *recherché*—faultless if you will. You don't despise these vanities—nor do I. I will go further and say that, in moderation, I enjoy them. But when Sir John Premium or Colonel Contango comes to dine with me, do you suppose that I could afford to regale them after this fashion? Lord bless your heart, why the cost of such a dinner would absorb a week's income! I attempt nothing of the kind. But they come nevertheless, and I need not add that the social success of a dinner party is not always in proportion to the expenditure involved. Of course it is absurd to pretend that the ordinary every-day fare would suffice on such occasions. It will not in any well-regulated household, and though I have no patience with people who content themselves with cold mutton *en famille* and give ostentatious banquets four or five times during the season, yet, as Charles Lamb puts it, enough is *not* as good as a feast.

But for all that there need not be extravagance— a little clear soup, a dish of fish, an entrée or two, a saddle of mutton, and a bit of game to follow, with a few sweets for the ladies, will make a dinner fit for a king. In these days one can get excellent wine at a moderate price if you know what's what, and where to order it. The selection of claret and port is not a question of science, nor is it always a question of money, but the result of a discriminating palate, which everyone does not possess.

It is astonishing what blind faith some men will put in brands, the dates of vintage, &c., &c., and it is a remarkable fact that at tables where such details are most earnestly discussed I have not unfrequently found the quality of the wine produced to be very so-so; whereas in other houses, where the contents of the bottles before you are not so much as mentioned, you may be imbibing nectar. I remember on one occasion that a distinguished general officer who was dining with us did me the honour to praise very highly some port from my cellar, and he even volunteered to guess its age. He may have been right for what I know, but if I had mentioned the price I gave for it (which I discreetly refrained from doing), I think the gallant soldier would have been surprised.

In a general way, of course, the *provenance*, so to speak, of wine is a suggestion of its excellence, but it is no guarantee. Even supposing that there has been no mistake in its authenticity—that the wine-grower, the importer, and the wine merchant are all above suspicion, a hundred accidents in storing or bottling, the state of the weather, the position of your cellar, and in claret especially the temperature of the room in which it is drunk, may make all the difference between a good and poor tap.

I often think that there is some analogy between the conventional value of wine and the conventional value of works of art. Your scientific critic in both cases may be devoid of taste. A picture which possesses an undoubted pedigree will often command admiration which is withheld from a better but unauthenticated example. '*If* that is a genuine Titian,' said an eminent amateur to me one day, as we were looking at an unknown canvas, 'it is a very fine thing!' Apart from the painter's name he could form no opinion on the work. I believe that a great many worthy people judge of pictures—and wine too—on this principle.

Dinners are often rendered tediously long and unwholesome by the introduction of 'courses' which are wholly unnecessary. Although I am quite aware that the preliminary *hors-d'œuvre* is a French fashion and sanctioned by tradition, I venture to think it might be abolished with advantage. What on earth is the use of stuffing yourself with caviar, sardines, radishes, and bread and butter, before you begin an ample meal? We are told that it is to whet the appetite. My answer is that people who require such a stimulant had far better wait until they are hungry. Besides, I don't believe that it ever had that effect. Whet the appetite, forsooth! It would certainly take mine away.

To give two kinds of soup, and two kinds of fish—whitebait perhaps excepted—is equally absurd. It involves much delay, and, while servants are dodging to and fro with the alternative dishes, both are likely to become cold. Try one soup and one fish, and you will find your guests quite content. If not, they ought to be.

From a gastronomic point of view I consider ices mere waste of money. In summer, perhaps, an iced pudding, or a dish of iced fruit which they call (Heaven knows why) *macédoine*, may be conceded to the ladies, but why, after this, frozen creams and congealed syrup should be served round to impair still further one's digestion I cannot understand. It is not only extremely unwholesome—as any medical man would tell you—but a positive insult to a good dinner.

Another preposterous custom is that of decanting champagne. What is the characteristic of this favourite wine? Assuredly its effervescing quality. Some people don't like effervescence even in soda-water. But no one opens a bottle of soda-water and waits until it has become flat before drinking it. If such people do not like effervescing wine, let them drink 'still' champagne. But to open a bottle of creaming épernay and pour it into a decanter before serving it is downright folly.

As to liqueurs, I hope I shall not offend the ladies when I suggest that they are altogether superfluous—indeed worse than superfluous to anyone with a refined palate. Children may enjoy a sip of green chartreuse, maraschino, noyeau, and so forth; but men and women who have had their share of wine at dinner, and are capable of appreciating a glass of good claret or port at dessert, should avoid the inevitable consequence of drinking liqueurs—hot syrupy stuff, after tasting which the finest Lafite is reduced to the level of mere *ordinaire.*

Personally I don't much care for condiments, but as most people take mustard with their beef, pepper with their peas, and so forth, it has often struck me as curious that at many luxurious tables the contents of the homely cruet stand should be so persistently ignored. They generally appear on the sideboard but are seldom handed round, and your shy guest never likes to ask for them. Another frequent and more serious omission is the biscuit box. Strawberries, candied fruit, pine-apple, chocolate creams, and what not are found in abundance. But the honest plain biscuit, a quite indispensable accompaniment to the after-dinner glass, is generally conspicuous by its absence.

In my dining-room we cannot conveniently seat more than fourteen at table, and I am rather glad of the restriction. In a small household, of course, where the reception of friends, even in a quiet way, entails some little trouble on the mistress, that good lady is naturally anxious to repay as much hospitality as possible within the scope of a single evening. Otherwise, and for the real pleasure of social intercourse, I regard *ten* as an ideal number, because it admits of general conversation. With twenty, or more, it becomes impossible. You talk to your neighbour on your right or left hand, but to no one else. The genial *raconteur*, no doubt, in these days has become obsolete. No individual guest is able to 'set the table on a roar.' It would be almost bad form to attempt it. But among intimate friends many a good story which might be admissible and entertaining in a party of ten or twelve is lost in the loud hum of conversation which prevails in a party of twenty.

Small dinner parties are, however, confessedly risky unless you get the right sort of people together. Indeed, the judicious assortment of guests is the one essential to success. Some hosts and hostesses are, I fear, strangely indifferent on this point. Others are unfortunate through force of circumstances. They set out with the best intentions, but owing to 'previous engagements' and consequent refusals, gaps are sure to occur in the little group of friends who were intended to meet. Those gaps must be filled up and possibly with less congenial spirits, and so a want of harmony may prevail. Supposing, for instance, the wife of a Conservative county member has to 'go down' with an advocate for Home Rule—or rattling Bob Wagsby is asked to 'take in' Miss Petronella Cramm, who distinguished herself so highly at Girton last term. Supposing my neighbour Lady Evangeline Bunyan, who, I feel convinced, is the anonymous donor of certain tracts which reach me once a fortnight, finds herself sitting next our ritualistic young curate, the Reverend Orphrey O'Stole, or my wife in a moment of indiscretion introduces the only dean we know to our young friend Mrs. Flyte, who dabbles in Theosophy —what untoward results may ensue!

To prevent these temporary but ill-fated *mésalliances* should be the effort of every cautious host. Sometimes, even with the utmost care, they cannot be prevented, or even foreseen. I remember on one occasion pairing off two guests at my table—one a good-looking, well-bred, and agreeable barrister, the other a still young, handsome, and highly cultured matron. I did not know that they had ever met before, and I made no doubt that each would be charmed with the other. But what was my disappointment and mortification to find whenever I looked towards them that they seemed mutually bored. They scarcely interchanged a word of conversation during dinner, and behaved, in short, like a couple of icebergs.

On investigating this phenomenon in the drawing-room afterwards I ascertained its cause. My guests had been neighbours at another table. The lady held advanced views on certain subjects and possessed but little sense of humour. The gentleman, though a brilliant talker, was somewhat given to raillery, especially on the matter of 'Women's rights.' He had resumed his bantering vein. She had become more and more serious. *Hinc illæ lacrymæ!* It was certainly unfortunate, but who could have foreseen such a result?

Sometimes it becomes a question whether it is better to promote a social duet between two guests of similar or of opposite temperament—to link together for a couple of hours the witty, the serious-minded, the shy, the forward, the intellectual, the frivolous, or *vice versâ* to associate them on what may be called an allopathic principle—so that one may serve as a foil for the other. I have known the latter experiment answer occasionally, but its success is not without exception, and the only escape from the dilemma is to give every person present a chance of opening a conversation *on both sides.* This can only be managed by preliminary introductions upstairs, and though I know this harmless custom has fallen into disuse, and that such presentations are considered unnecessary, because in the great world everyone is supposed to know everyone else, we in humble circles must be quite aware that this is a mere fiction. Indeed, a clever, tactful hostess cannot spend what is called the *mauvais quart d'heure* in her drawing-room better than by bringing people together before dinner. It involves a little trouble of course, but the result achieved is well worth the pains. It gives every guest a double chance of talking at table, and that is a great gain; for a dinner party where anyone sits mum may be regarded as a failure.

Beyond repeating my faith in a moderate *menu,* I shall not attempt to offer any suggestions as to the character and quality of the dishes which it includes. Why they are still described in a foreign language is a mystery past my comprehension. In the early part of this century there may have been a reason for it, because French cookery was then superior to our own. But it is not so now, at least in domestic life. Assuming the same expense in each case, you may dine nowadays as well in London as you do in Paris. Why, therefore, should we not have an *English* bill of fare? Why should we adopt the wretched jargon of 'rosbif' and 'plombuden' in describing our national dishes? Don't you think a 'fore-quarter of lamb' sounds quite as inviting as *un quartier d'agneau*? The only serious difference I ever have with my wife on these occasions is on that point. I am for the Anglican usage, and I had nearly converted her to my opinion when she asked me satirically what was the English for *suprême de volaille*. I confess that I could not translate it into my mother tongue, and consequently she triumphed.

Young housewives talk a great deal of nonsense about *modes* of cooking, but except in the case of a few complex and exceptional dishes, there are but two modes, the right and the wrong. The real secret of excellence in this, as in all other arts, is experience. In private life I have heard some heretics aver that they can 'eat anything'—that is to say, that *en famille* they keep a slipslop, indifferent, or niggardly table, which means that they either have the digestion of an ostrich, or else that they incur doctor's bills unnecessarily. Such people miss a great deal of harmless pleasure—may suffer greatly from dyspepsia and consequent ill temper. If you feed—I cannot say dine—at their houses you will regret it. But if you insist on having dishes sent up properly for your family dinner—if you are particular about roasting and boiling—if you take care to be supplied with meat of the best quality, wholesomely prepared vegetables and sauces; if, in short, your tradesmen know that you are not to be imposed upon, and if your cook's hand is kept in constant practice, your friends will find no fault with the occasional feast.

And now, if you please, we will go upstairs and join the ladies.

CHAPTER III

OUR DRAWING-ROOM

The staircase is rather a 'feature' in my house. It is wider and better lighted than in most tenements of the same size, but its plan is peculiar, not to say inconvenient. Generally speaking, there are two flights of stairs between the ground and first floor. Here there is but one and a graduated landing. You walk out of the drawing-room floor on to a flat, but you have scarcely taken three paces before you drop down six inches to a lower level. A yard or so further on you drop down again, and so on till you turn the corner, where there are three steps, and you find yourself on another landing. It is here that the fun begins, for the rest of the staircase descends in a rapid slope, and if you happen to be walking just behind Mrs. Trainly Peacock's long skirt, it is advisable to hold well on by the handrail, or you may reach the dining-room door more quickly than you anticipated, and possibly head foremost. It never happened to myself; but then I am a careful man, and know the ways of the house very well.

I do *not* know the architect who designed it, but if by chance these lines should ever meet his eye, I hope he may have lived long enough to see the errors of his youth. I call it an error charitably, but a suspicion has more than once crossed my mind that he may have been on friendly terms with some surgeon in this neighbourhood. It is certain that the houses in Dexter Square present unusual opportunities for practice in the way of bone-setting.

Nevertheless the staircase, on the whole, is satisfactory in appearance. Its walls afford a convenient space for pictures which I cannot hang elsewhere. There are water-colour sketches in Switzerland, France, Belgium, and Italy, but as they are chiefly productions of my own brush I shall modestly refrain from describing them. You may, however, be attracted by a painting executed nearly four centuries ago, the work of Michele da Verona, and representing a group of mounted soldiers taking leave of their womankind on the eve of a battle. The warriors, it must be confessed, do not present a very heroic appearance, and my friend Banterfield, who has no reverence for antiquity, asked me one day whether the features and expression of one of them did not remind me of Sam Weller's father. The ladies of the party, too, are of that type which may be described as 'intense' rather than beautiful, but then they are arrayed in a sort of pseudo-classical costume which compensates in dignity for what they want in grace. As for the chargers on which the cavalry are mounted, I have seldom seen any four-footed creatures out of Noah's Ark so supremely comical. My wife's maid told her that they attracted the notice of Snaffle, our groom, one morning as he was carrying a portmanteau upstairs, and that, viewing the animals from a professional point of view, he could not conceal his scorn.

'Call that a 'oss, Miss Phyllis!' observed the expert; 'why there ain't a butcher in Bayswater who would care to give a fifpun' note for sich a screw; and if the picter's four 'undred years old, they must have 'ad queer notions of a mount in those days! I don't think much of the young women neither, but there, what can you expect o' gals who'd keep company with a lot of militiamen?'

Opposite this work of art, and carefully enclosed in a glass case, hangs a curious specimen of mediæval embroidery—part of some ecclesiastical vestment—which I bought in Siena more than twenty-five years ago; and near it is a drawing I made of Niccolo Pisano's famous pulpit in the cathedral of that beautiful and ancient city. I remember spending a fortnight over the work, returning to it day after day with unceasing interest. It was an elaborate and troublesome job to get the background of groined vaulting in right perspective, but I enjoyed it. What an age ago it seems! '*Olim meminisse*,' &c., &c. I doubt whether I should have patience enough to make such a drawing now.

My staircase is lighted by three windows of ample size which surround the landing, and if you have a taste for flowers painted on glass, the ornamental borders of each sash may be studied as brilliant examples of all that should be avoided in decorative art. I have often thought of removing them, but have been deterred from doing so, partly out of consideration for my landlord, but chiefly, I confess, by motives of economy. My scruples, however, are being overcome by our good housemaid, Susan, who considerately manages to break one of the panes about once a month, and in these circumstances I feel amply justified in replacing it with plain glass. I calculate that on the expiration of my lease all the painted panes will have disappeared. If I remain in the house, I shall do so with a clear conscience, and if I don't, the next tenant will have much to be grateful for.

I do not, however, contemplate all of Susan's accidents with the same equanimity. When, for instance, in the course of her dusting operations, she endeavoured to reach a top shelf in my bookcase by standing on an inverted china bowl, which succumbed to her weight and was smashed to atoms on the floor, or when, under plea of cleaning my best specimen of Venetian glass, she plunged it into a tub of boiling water and was surprised to hear it 'go crack'; when she endeavoured to clean the gilding of an ancient picture-frame by a generous use of yellow soap and soda, and when she laid a piece of choice Oriental embroidery with its face downwards on a newly polished table (to keep it, as she said, from the dust), I must admit that I lost my temper. But these were the errors of youth and inexperience. She is more careful now. Out of my last two dozen hock glasses I have at least fifteen left, and I don't think the sash lines snap *quite* so frequently as they did.

As a rule, servants have an accommodating way of sharing between them the blame which attaches to breakages. Thus, when Susan hits one of the gas-globes with a step ladder she expresses great regret, but cheerfully adds that it is *only* cracked and will last for years. A fortnight later the same globe comes to pieces in Mary's hands, but then, as she justly remarks, it was cracked ever so long ago, and 'was bound to go, pleassir, *some* time if you was as gentle as a lamb with it.' As master of the house I find it extremely difficult to answer these arguments, and, on the principle of 'the less said the better,' I usually restrict myself to monosyllables more or less emphatic.

In summer my wife, who is very fond of flowers, makes the staircase gay with geraniums, calceolarias, marguerites, and mignonette. They give a little trouble in the way of daily watering, leaf-picking, &c., and add something to the monthly bills, but, after all, it does not amount to more than a few pounds a year, and, to my mind, the money is well spent. What is a town house without flowers? Not all the elegant furniture, gorgeous brocades, or costly *bric-à-brac* which a wealthy connoisseur can assemble under one roof will charm the eye like a country garden, and we, whom an unkindly fate rarely allows to set foot in one, may be thankful for the honest industry which fills our florists' shops with customers, and decks the dull windows of many a London street. A few conservatory stands filled with evergreens, a majolica pedestal here and there crowned with a pretty bowpot, a solanum plant inserted in a terra-cotta vase, a bunch of daffodils in a Venetian beaker, are, after all, inexpensive luxuries, and help to *égayer* many a modest home. Pictures, bronzes, marbles, and old china may be delightful in their way, but it is not everyone who can afford to buy them. Flowers and flowering shrubs are within reach of most purses. '*All a-blowing, a-growing!*' Hark! there is the botanical pedlar bawling out his variegated ware as he pushes his truck before him down the street. Let us hail him and buy a hyacinth for the mantelpiece.

In the season my wife's smart friends are pleased to compliment her on the appearance of our staircase, and, to say the truth, it looks more cheerful than many which she sees during a round of calls on people whose income must be five times as much as ours. A little pains, a little sense of the picturesque, a little love of home life will often go as far as a big cheque in housekeeping. It is a very old and hackneyed question how far wealth increases one's happiness, and I am not going to moralise about it. The enjoyment of money I suppose mainly depends upon two questions: first, how it is acquired, and, secondly, how it is spent. To pass from narrow circumstances to comfort is a great gain in every sense—morally, physically, and socially. Few things are more humiliating than the painful minuteness of needful economy. The man who has to look twice at every shilling before he lays it down, who is perpetually worried by the consideration whether he can afford this or that trifle, is apt to grow mean and small-minded. To rise from this state to that of easy competence; to be able to keep a fair balance at one's bankers', to have enough for oneself and a little more to spare for others—that indeed is worth a struggle in the great battle of life, and those who win their way to such a condition are to be congratulated. But, having arrived at this goal, to plod wearily on toiling and moiling for more and more money, and allowing the attainment of that object to absorb one's energies—to sacrifice health, spirits, family affection, the cultivation of taste and easy leisure for the sake of amassing riches—is a career which no one need envy. You might as well be a galley-slave in golden chains.

As for those who live on what is called an 'unearned increment,' I cannot pretend to judge, having had little or no experience in that line, but I can truly say that if my patrimony had been a large one I should have missed a great deal of simple pleasure in housekeeping. The happy bride and bridegroom who return after a month's tour in Scotland or the Italian lakes to their mansion in Belgravia, which has been fitted up by those eminent decorators Messrs. Brocas & Gildwell, at a cost of say five thousand pounds, look round and admire no doubt, but can hardly take much interest in their surroundings.

Those elegant appointments represent no individual taste, no long-deferred wishes, no nice calculations of cost, no lucky bargains or gradual rises in the scale of comfort. The owners have acquired satiety too soon; there is nothing left to desire. They have discounted the greater part of their pleasure.

When we first set up an establishment it was a small flat in Bloomsbury, and I suppose our first outlay in furniture did not exceed 500*l*. In those days it was difficult—almost impossible—to buy even a chiffonier of decent design. Every article partaking of what is now called 'artistic' taste had to be made expressly and at an extravagant price, not because it was elaborate in workmanship, but because it was unusual in form. Until we could afford more luxurious seats, I remember that we furnished our dining-room with 'windsor' chairs, which I preserve to this day—in my kitchen. The construction of our tables, bookcases, &c., was entrusted to an intelligent cabinet-maker, and their progress watched with vast interest. Our window curtains were selected after long consultation as the only tolerable specimens of textile work among a heap of horrors. The fitting up of our mantelpieces was the result of deep study. The choice of wall-papers and carpets kept us in a state of enjoyable excitement. How delighted we were to find a dinner service of a tolerable pattern! The arrival of our sofa was quite an event.

As year by year we haunted sale-rooms and picked up bargains in the way of marquetry, blue china, and old metal-work, every fresh acquisition was a source of joy to us—something to anticipate, something to talk about, something to love and enjoy when we got it. We furnished our home, in short, by degrees, and every addition to its contents marked a little epoch in our experience.

Now, supposing that, instead of this, some beneficent fairy—or wealthy ancestor—had given us the means to indulge in lavish expenditure just as we were starting in life, and we had been popped down all at once in a house crowded with luxuries, what a deal of amusement we should have lost. For this reason, among many others, I am thankful to a kindly fate that I was not born a rich man. If ever I should become one, may I keep a light heart!

'Det vitam: det opes: æquum mi animum ipse parabo.'

As I pass up or down my staircase the sketches on the walls recall pleasant memories of many a summer holiday. That view from the ivy- and clematis-clad arbour, looking on the lovely lake of Thun with the pyramidal Niesen in the distance, the red-roofed, picturesque, old town itself, in bright sunlight under a blue sky, reminds me of a pleasant fortnight in the hospitable Bellevue Hotel. That sturdy brick arch, through which one sees a lengthy vista of marble fish-stalls and a quaintly shadowed alley, was sketched in the Ghetto at Rome many, many years ago. They tell me that the Pescheria has been long pulled down, and that the walls of the Coliseum, thickly covered, when I saw them last, with overhanging foliage and creepers, are now shaved as clean as a billiard ball. Here is an old half-timbered cottage before which I sat down at Rochefort in Belgium during our stay in the Ardennes, and there is a bit of the ancient *fossé* which surrounds the walls of Dinan. That village scene, with the peasant girl riding down the street on a tall sleek mule, and rustic laundry-women kneeling over the conduit, occupied me for several happy mornings at Evolena in the Val d'Herens. The drawing just above it represents a church porch in the neighbourhood of Locarno, and the *contadina* sitting in its shade was, if the truth must be told, painted from a young English lady who good-naturedly donned that humble costume and posed as my model.

Souvenirs of France, Germany, and Belgium—impressions of scenery in the Salzkammergut and the Pyrenees—effects of light and shade in Scotland, blots of colour in Wales, and studies of foliage in the New Forest—here they all hang side by side, relics of a harmless industry which, if unprofitable in a financial sense, has at least given me a vast deal of pleasure. A man who carries a sketch-book and can fill it with tolerable studies during his excursions has, I fancy, a certain advantage over his fellow tourists. Travelling itself is all very well for a while, but as you move from place to place looking at fresh scenery every day—lakes, mountains, waterfalls, woodland, rushing rivers, pasture-land, and snow-fields—as you hasten through town after town, inspecting cathedrals, museums, *piazze*, and palaces, confess now, don't you find the whole business rather wearisome after a fortnight? Isn't it rather a relief when you arrive at a place where there is no church to examine and no pictures to criticise? What a deal of perfunctory work we discharge under the name of sightseeing! And then the hurry and bustle of the whole affair. Half your time is spent in packing and unpacking—settling hotel bills, catching trains, and what not. How can one enjoy such a holiday? There is no leisure, no repose, no comfort in touring.

I protest that if anyone undertook to frank me on a journey round the world free of charge, on condition that I should never remain more than two days in the same place, I would not accept the offer. No; give me six weeks' leave with an alpenstock, a sketch-book, and permission to divide the time between a mountain valley in Switzerland, a comfortable hotel on one of the Italian lakes, and a fortnight's stay at Venice or Perugia, and I will undertake to enjoy myself—weather permitting.

But we have been dawdling too long on the staircase. Let us pass through that door on the left and enter the drawing-room. It is not a very large one, and certainly not big enough for what house-agents describe as 'purposes of reception.' It might hold about thirty people—all told—with convenience. More would certainly crowd it. In our younger days, when we followed the practice of our betters and attempted an occasional 'At Home,' I am ashamed to remember how many guests we invited to assemble in that room—how they overflowed down the staircase on to the balconies and even into the dining-room below. It is certainly an inexpensive mode of paying off social obligations, and I find that even people of affluence are not deterred by their wealth from indulging in this form of economy. A few quarts of tea and coffee (with the massive family plate of course *en évidence*), a dozen or so of champagne—or that dangerous mixture known as claret-cup—a modest supply of mayonnaise, parsley-decked sandwiches, and ices *ad libitum*, six ex-butlers or hired waiting-women behind the buffet, and a linkman bawling out for carriages at the door, do not, after all, represent a very large outlay of income, and I have known these simple elements of hospitality form the basis of what is popularly regarded as an entertainment. But the follies of my youth are now abandoned. I hate 'crushes,' and unless I am dining out elsewhere, never go to evening parties. Consequently we never give them, and as a lounge for a few friends my drawing-room does very well.

The room is simply, but I hope prettily, furnished —so at least my friends are pleased to say. That velvet-covered settle is copied from one in the long gallery at Knole Park, and the chairs are an attempt to combine the comfortable with the picturesque. Those mantel-piece mirrors date from an early period—I mean the first days of our housekeeping—and though they are out of fashion now, I keep them for old association's sake, and because they brighten up the room. The glazed cabinet is filled with lucky bargains picked up for years past on the Continent and London sale-rooms —old china, Venetian glass, and a hundred nick-nacks. That ebonised chiffonier between the windows is panelled with plaques of bristol-board overlaid with Italian needlework at least two centuries old. They represent the mythical adventures of one Bertoldo, a naughty boy, who may be seen riding backwards on a donkey, hiding in a furnace, carried up into the air by cranes, and taking part in a score of wonderful adventures too numerous to detail. Each panel is inscribed with a distich from an old Florentine ballad describing the incident represented. There are four-and-twenty scenes, some of them full of humour, and reminding one of Caldecott's designs.

In the days of my childhood a large round table was considered indispensable in every English drawing-room. Except in old-fashioned houses one never sees such a thing nowadays. In its place are substituted three or four small circular tables which upholsterers call 'occasional,' though what they occasion, unless it is accidents when upset, I have never been able to see.

On these pieces of furniture my wife is pleased to pile books, newspapers, flower-pots, work-baskets, and photograph stands in such an ingenious manner that it is difficult to remove one article without disturbing the rest. It is almost like a game of 'Spellicans' on a large scale, and only constant practice enables me to play it successfully. For my own part I generally lose not only the game, but my temper, and all this comes of not understanding the requirements of a fashionable drawing-room.

I can't say much for the piano, and, judging from the volume of sound which reaches our ears from a rival instrument next door, I should say that ours was not quite so noisy as my neighbour's. But whether that is an advantage or not I do not presume to judge, for taste differs so much on these matters, and I am not what is called a musical man. Once a month a gentle-looking youth comes to tune it, and is received with great joy by our little terrier 'Pixie, who barks during the whole performance if he is not locked up elsewhere, a fact which I believe has seriously affected the quality of the bass notes.

The walls of our drawing-room are hung with water-colour drawings and a few copies from the old masters. Among the latter I chiefly prize a reproduction of Botticelli's well-known 'tondo' in the Uffizi Gallery at Florence, representing the Virgin and Child surrounded by angels, and another equally good copy of his 'Prima Vera.' In these two wonderful designs we may admire, I think, all that is most lovely and attractive in this gifted painter's work, and at the same time recognise the two great influences which inspired his hand. They are widely removed in aim and essence from each other, one breathing that spirit of devotion and saintly grace which, in art and literature at least, characterised mediæval Christianity; the other instinct with the love of life, of freedom, of intellectual exercise and physical beauty which we associate with the Renaissance. Filipepi, no doubt, sincerely felt both in turn: hesitated as we know between them, and it is to this fortunate vacillation that the world owes one of the most beautiful religious pictures and one of the most interesting allegories ever portrayed.

It would be too much to expect all the ladies who share my wife's five o'clock tea to appreciate these works, which I find they describe as 'quaint,' 'præ-Raphaelite,' 'curious,' 'ritualistic,' or 'comical' as the spirit moves them. But there is in the same room another treasure of pictorial art which interests them vastly, because it represents a betrothal, a subject always sure to awaken sympathy in the female mind, whether depicted on canvas or recorded in the 'Morning Post.'

The work in question is a miniature painting, evidently by a French or Flemish artist of the 16th century. The young couple stand side by side, clad in the costume of the period, and about to join hands. The features of each wear an expression of intense respect, but to a modern eye rather too serious to denote enthusiasm. The bridegroom is somewhat priggish in appearance, and the lady is only fairly good-looking, but the emblems by which they are surrounded leave no doubt as to their affection. Above the pair are two hearts intertwined in a true lovers' knot, a device suggestive of the 14th of February when valentines were in vogue. The scene is enriched by a border of marigolds and pansies, very cleverly painted, and in the background are inscribed, in old French, various verses of an amatory nature. The following is a specimen :—

'Soulcy d'Amour en ma doulce pensée
heureusement a sorty son effaict,
puisque tu m'as ta grace dispensée
et ton vouloir pareil au mien est faict,
Le bien d'Amour monstre l'effaict parfaict.

> 'En jouyssant de la vie amoureuse
> parfaicte amour de Vertu vigoreuse
> faict a nous deux ses gracieux accords :
> Et au soulcy de la pensée heureuse
> Vindrent deux cœurs, deux âmes et deux corps.'

The frame which encloses this little picture is in itself a work of art. It is of cinque-cento design with a column on either side, resting on a plinth and supporting an entablature, both elaborately enriched with gilt bas-reliefs, in which *amorini*, fruit and flowers are introduced, while in the tympanum of an arched pediment above is a finely modelled figure of Ceres, reclining in a cornfield.

This is our latest and favourite toy, and in order to protect the gilding we have placed it in a glass case. Alack, alack! what children we all are! Three hundred years ago it was the plaything of other fools, perhaps the two lovers whose portraits I have just described. How did they fare, I wonder, in wedlock? Was that *grace dispensée* doled out habitually or did the supply run short after a while? *Soulcy d'Amour* and *doulces pensées* are all very well in a honeymoon, but when the business of life begins, those flowers of romance (for you will perceive the poet's punning allusion to pansies and marigolds) no longer symbolise the thoughts and cares which are uppermost in the minds of most mortals. There is the world before us, with ambition, duty, social obligations, family claims, the necessity for work perhaps, or the love of pleasure, all pulling us different ways: and we yield in this direction or that as our several temperaments, or the Fates, decree.

It would interest me vastly to know the names of these young people, where they settled down, whether they lived to grow old, how many children, if any, survived them, and what has become of their descendants. I should like to trace out any existing members of the family, and show them this picture of their ancestors, who, for what I know, may have intended it as an heirloom to be handed down from generation to generation. And lo! three centuries after it was painted, here it is among aliens in a modern London drawing-room.

Once a week, when it pleases my wife to call herself 'At Home,' her friends rally round her in this apartment. I am seldom present on those festive occasions, but I am given to understand that our best silver teapot has to be replenished several times between four and six o'clock; that cake, bread and butter, and biscuits are in constant requisition, that most of the guests stay an hour or so, and that conversation never flags. With regard to the latter fact, I can readily believe—and I speak from personal experience—that my wife would set an excellent example, and indeed it seems a wise provision of nature that women who are sent into this world to cheer and solace us, and who are debarred by various causes from taking much physical exercise, should be possessed of such remarkable energy as talkers.

Take, for instance, my dear friend Lady Clacke Millington, who will entertain you for the best part of an afternoon with her artless prattle. It is not that what she says shows much erudition or even humour, but then there is so much of it—such an unceasing flow of language. She is never at a loss for a word. It is wonderful.

Again, there is my wife's Scotch cousin, Mrs. McJauleigh, whose powers of verbal amplification are such, that one out of her vast *répertoire* of anecdotes would fill a chapter in this volume. There is nothing too trival, nothing too abstruse to be included in her narrative. She omits no details, and I have known her to correct herself twice respecting the day of the week on which an apparently unimportant circumstance occurred, so anxious is she always to be accurate in telling her good stories. It is a great virtue, that of accuracy in conversation, and it helps to while away the time so! When Mrs. McJauleigh gets me into a convenient corner, I am, so to speak, absorbed. I can talk to no one else. Partly on this account, because it would seem rude to confine one's attention to a particular guest, and partly because our male friends rarely come to five o'clock teas, I modestly refrain from attending them myself, and thus the ladies have it all their own way.

Among other advantages it gives them an excellent opportunity to admire each other's dresses; to recount (of course in confidence) the wonderful bargains which they struck at Blackwood's recent sale in the Avenue; how that lovely mantle, of which the original price was ten guineas (so the shopman said), came to be acquired for six; why that charming hat, which was sent as a pattern straight from Paris only two months ago, was purchased by its happy owner at half its proper cost; and where elegant boots of the very best manufacture can be obtained at an absurdly cheap rate, simply because their heels are only two inches high, the present fashion requiring an elevation of three from the ground.

Among the married ladies, no doubt, some of the conversation turns on family matters, as, for instance, the cutting of dear baby's teeth; Bob's recent vaccination; Lucy's attack of measles; Harry's first experiences at Rugby; Sylvia's success at Girton, and what not. And here let me say in a parenthesis, that if the result of what is called the 'higher education' of women be half as beneficial as our modern reformers anticipate, British wives and mothers in the next generation will be very remarkable members of society.

Every department of 'culture'—art, literature, science, and moral philosophy—has been thrown open to them in girlhood. What a rich harvest of intellectual fruit this ought to bear hereafter! One wonders sometimes how, in the midst of their multifarious studies, these fair graduates will find time, or, indeed, feel inclination, for the humdrum functions of daily life, for household duties, for nursery cares, for friendly intercourse and domestic sympathy. Will they ever condescend to such homely offices as ordering the dinner, looking after their servants, keeping the rooms tidy, watching by the bed of a sick child, or cheering the bread-winner when he comes back after a hard day's work? Perhaps some may be found who, while maintaining their high intellectual standard, will not neglect these feminine pleasures and obligations, but, at present, men who have arrived at the age of fogeydom may be excused for feeling a little doubtful on that point.

Meanwhile, let us ask ourselves, what has been the immediate result of this education craze. Has it made our girls generally more agreeable, more modest, more useful, more unselfish, more dutiful, or more attractive than their mothers? Of the hundreds who, year by year, carry off high school prizes, pass local examinations and win scholarships, how many turn their erudition to account? In their insatiable thirst for knowledge, some of them, I fancy, have imbibed but little of the milk of human kindness. Amid their devotion to the arts, not a few have left the graces unheeded.

The study of quadratic equations may be all very well, but, for my part, I would rather that my daughter had mastered the mysteries of plain stitching. It seems flat heresy to say so, but I cannot help thinking it more important that she should be a good housewife than be able to remember the agrarian laws of Spurius Cassius.

To be intelligent, to have a bright sense of humour —which means a quick perception and a kindly heart —to be affectionate and respectful to her elders, sympathetic to the young, patient and amiable to her inferiors, to be discreet, methodical, and zealous in the management of her home: these are the qualities which, if we spoke truly, most of us prize in a woman, and which will secure more happiness to herself and those about her, than if she had studied a dozen treatises on geology, and learned enough Greek to read Plato without a crib.

Five o'clock teas supply to the ladies the same sort of social intercourse among themselves which a man gets at his club, and it would be selfish to begrudge them an afternoon, once a week let us say during the season, to meet each other, exchange ideas, and indulge in a little harmless gossip. There is a vulgar notion that at these re-unions a great deal of scandal is retailed. That I believe to be an unfounded calumny. Time was, no doubt, when Mrs. Candour and Lady Sneerwell said their say in London drawing-rooms, and found a ready audience among 'people of quality.' But, thank goodness, Society has undergone great changes since Sheridan's day, and ladies of fashion no longer meet to slander their fair neighbours. Apart from the moral aspects of the question, it would be considered bad form. Ill-natured innuendoes are now no more tolerated among well-bred women than dubious stories among gentlemen after dinner. There must be old folks, and smart old folks too, of both sexes, still living, who remember those odious customs, and preserve a wise reticence over the follies and bad taste of their youth. I don't suppose we are much wiser or more virtuous than our ancestors, but at least we have learnt to govern our tongues.

So let us hope that no mischief or malice is whispered in our drawing-room. Perhaps the conversation is not very learned or edifying, but ladies, like ourselves, do not want to be always instructed, and, for my own part, I think a female prig is worse than a male one, which is saying a great deal. In these solemn days of culture let us be thankful that we have some leisure left for small talk and frivolity. Great heavens!

what a dreary world this would be without a little idleness and merriment! The judicious goodwife who welcomes her husband's friends round her little tea table now and then does him an inestimable service, and indeed it is the only way in which a circle of acquaintance, whether useful or ornamental, can be properly kept up. Abolish five o'clock 'at homes,' and Society will soon forget you. I have no patience with women who say that they have no time for calling on each other. A man might as well urge that he has no time for exercise. Both are necessary for a healthy life.

But our drawing-room is not always full. In the morning that old-fashioned bureau sees a deal of work done; letters written, accounts examined, household matters considered, daily orders given, invitations received or dispatched, new books cut open, maps consulted, dictionaries turned over, pens, ink, and paper usefully employed.

Sometimes the flower-pots want replenishing, and one comes home to find the room gay with gems from Covent Garden or the neighbouring florist. Sometimes the china requires washing; sometimes the furniture has to be rubbed up, or the pictures need dusting. The eyes of the mistress, if not her hands, are necessary for all these little domestic cares, and she who entrusts such work entirely to her servants is either an idle or a foolish one.

I fancy there is more energy required in the management of a small household than we bearded creatures, who rush away every day after breakfast to our offices, our chambers, or our studios, generally realise. If 'man goeth forth to his work and to his labour until the evening,' the women whom he leaves at home are not idle.

Here would be a famous opportunity for moralising on the duties of a wife, but that, as every married man knows, is dangerous ground. We will assume, therefore, that by 8 o'clock P.M. we are all satisfied with ourselves and our belongings—down to the cook—at Terra-cottage, and if that is so, it will be pleasant after dinner to sit round the drawing-room fireplace for a quiet chat, or listen as some one reads aloud a smart article in our favourite review or a cheery novel, just to keep us all awake until bedtime.

CHAPTER IV

OUR 'LITTLE ONES'

If I had to give a cursory and concise definition of Terra-cottage, I should describe it as the Paradise of Pets. Small domestic quadrupeds of one kind or another have been established there for years past, and during their successive lives have reigned supreme over the whole establishment, sometimes as single and absolute monarchs, sometimes adopting the principle of a dual government, occasionally lapsing into an oligarchy, but always exercising complete sway over their human subjects, and exacting from them an obedience and devotion which have rarely, if ever, faltered.

It would be difficult to assign any particular date to the origin of this system of administration. The first ruler concerning whose life any authentic particulars are recorded was a toy Maltese pup, named, probably from the silky texture of his snow-white coat, 'Fluffy,' who ascended the throne, or rather was lifted on to the best easy chair, at a very youthful age. He was adored by the household, who vied with each other in ministering to his comforts, and providing him with dainty food and amusements suitable to his years, or, to speak more correctly, his *months.* Being of a frail constitution, it was naturally thought probable that ordinary canine fare might disagree with him. Accordingly chicken wings and milk, sopped sponge cakes, and other refined delicacies formed his principal diet, which he consumed with amazing relish and a lofty disregard for the conventional decorum of artificial life, more especially with respect to crumbs. He evinced an intelligent interest in his mistress's household duties—assisted her in the daily function of ordering dinner with such assiduity that he has been known to tumble down the kitchen stairs in the hasty prosecution of this object, and never failed when he had a chance to inspect the contents of the larder, where his curiosity was raised to a greater height than his front paws, which only reached to the lowest shelf. He was an amiable and affectionate creature if the outward and visible signs of puppy-pleasure may be trusted. But to say that he wagged his tail would be an empty compliment. It had been docked so short in infancy that it positively vibrated with delight—and he was never known to squeal except when his claws got entangled with his coat, or when a dinner guest occasionally mistook him for a footstool under the table.

Unfortunately these endearing characteristics

were not accompanied by much depth of intellect. Fluffy was, it must be confessed, of a very frivolous disposition. His habit of climbing over the parlourmaid's ankles during family prayers—even after having been carefully consigned to his basket—cannot be excused, and though a spirit of inquiry and investigation is perhaps natural to youth, it would hardly justify his endeavouring to scatter the contents of the coal-box on the drawing-room hearth-rug as a means of athletic exercise.

Whether his daily regimen palled upon his appetite or whether his taste became perverted through premature self-indulgence we never could understand, but certain it is that before he had arrived at maturity, he had developed an abnormal craving for strange and unwholesome articles of diet, ranging from half-knitted woollen socks to best screened Wallsend. During these gastronomical experiments he one day unhappily selected for his lunch a sherry cork, which proved too much for his digestion, and cut short a career which will always live in our memory.

Fluffy was a pure-bred dog, and under an impression that the southern blood which he inherited was a cause of delicacy in his constitution we determined that his successor should be of a hardier sort.

It so happened that about this time a highly respected cabman, with a turn for zoology, who resided in a neighbouring mews, brought to us a litter of pups accompanied by their mother, a native of Scotland, whose late husband had been of Maltese origin. They were fat little creatures, chiefly remarkable for their thick, curly, white coats and unsophisticated manners. There was not much to choose between them, but we selected the liveliest and dismissed the rest of the family.

The Scotch widow, finding herself in the entrance hall with only four out of five of her little ones, looked uneasy, counted them again to make quite sure, and at first was for bolting back into the dining-room to reclaim her missing infant. But after a little moral persuasion and the free gift of a mutton-chop bone, she took a philosophical view of her domestic bereavement and trotted off at the cabman's heels.

Our new pet was christened 'Mopsy,' but in course of time the name became corrupted into 'Mossy,' and finally settled down into 'Moss.' He was very small when he first came to us—so small that the exertion of barking frequently capsized him; but as he grew older he developed longitudinally, like a pocket telescope. He had a fine white coat and a beautiful head, which I suspect he inherited from his papa, with large black eyes as brilliant as an onyx, but the proportions of his body were not satisfactory, and, if the truth must be told, somewhat plebeian.

Whatever deficiencies were observable, however, in his physical appearance, were more than redeemed by his moral nature. I use the word moral in its widest sense, because to this day I am still in doubt whether good or evil most predominated in his disposition. But he certainly was a dog of great character. Having foreseen in early youth the personal inconvenience which would ensue from his being called on to perform any canine tricks, he steadily refused to learn any; made believe that he was too weak in the spine to stand begging, and when we gave him a stick to carry let it drop out of his mouth with an absent air, as if he didn't know what we meant. He also shammed deafness when it suited his purpose, and the only whistle he ever paid attention to was one at the end of a whip. In reality he was wonderfully intelligent, and not only learned to discriminate between a coaxing voice and a scolding voice, but was particularly sensitive to ridicule or any imputation of disgrace.

He lived in a little wicker house which he kept in great order, carefully shaking up the mat to ensure comfort in his afternoon nap, and looking out from the door with the conscious pride of possession; but if he were peremptorily sent there by way of punishment, he regarded it in the light of an insult. There is not much difference in the sound of the words 'biscuit!' and 'basket!' The former would set his tail wagging, but it stopped the moment he heard the latter, which was the signal for his retreat.

He conceived a deep-rooted aversion to two objects, one was my umbrella, and the other a book of family photographs. In the first instance his dislike may be attributed to the fact that I found the umbrella ferrule useful when he lingered unnecessarily during our walks (for being a lazy dog I made a point of taking him out every morning for a constitutional), but why he hated the photograph book so bitterly I could never understand. The very sight of it threw him into a fury—and if Moss had a weak point it was temper.

It was wonderful that a really harmless dog (for he was never known to bite man, woman, or child) should get into such frightful passions. A few words of sharp reproof would raise his indignation to such a height that he positively chattered with rage. It was neither a bark, nor a howl, nor a whine, but the sounds which he uttered on these occasions were the nearest approach to canine swearing that I ever heard, and his expression for the time was positively malignant.

But his anger did not last long. After a few minutes' retirement in his basket he would come out again, very penitent, and heartily ashamed of himself. For, with all his bad temper, Mr. Moss was an affectionate little creature, and so devoted to his mistress that he positively pined away one autumn when she was away from home some weeks longer than usual.

Among four-footed companions he contracted more than one friendship during his career. He was on excellent terms with the family cat, and took such a lively interest in her domestic troubles that we generally saved one kitten from each litter to be his special playmate. The delight which he evinced at the fresh advent of each little stranger never palled. He would bark and caper round it with the utmost glee as it lay sprawling on the hearth-rug; then stop breathless to watch its movements, and presently dart forward and seize the little creature's leg or tail in his mouth, but always with the most tender care and gentleness. Mistress Pussy, who came to regard him in the light of a privileged godfather, used to sit watching their antics with supreme satisfaction, and —though she disliked dogs in general—placed unbounded confidence in Mr. Moss.

Female cats no doubt are very interesting, but the interest in them culminates, if I may venture so to put it, too frequently, and the duty of providing a comfortable home or a watery grave two or three times a year for half a dozen limp little purblind squealing creatures is really a heavy responsibility, from which the inhabitants of Terra-cottage naturally shrink. So we incline to Toms, and so long as they are respectably conducted (as they generally are) indoors, we don't trouble ourselves much about their morals elsewhere.

We have had some delightful Toms. There was 'Parker' (so called from the fact of his having been found while a wee kitten in Kensington Gardens). He used to sit on my shoulder at breakfast time, answer with a sort of chirrupy mew when he was called, scratched all the dining-room chairs with strict impartiality, and attained amazing skill in the capture of buzzing flies.

There was 'Sandy,' whose lovely yellow-brown coat was the envy of all the cats in the neighbourhood, a splendid mouser, but he only hunted for amusement and never deigned to eat his prey. Indeed, so delicate was he in his diet that he has been known to turn aside from yesterday's milk with an air of disdain, and, fond as he was of fish, he never could bring himself to taste red-herring. Sandy was, in short, an epicure, and, if the truth must be told, somewhat of a rake. Some excuse may be urged on the ground of his youth and the dangerous attractiveness of his exterior, but nothing can palliate the indiscriminate gallantry of his conduct and the heedless disregard of principle, which made him at once the adoration and the terror of his neighbours.

I have seen five lady-cats sitting in watch for him (and pretending not to see each other) in the square garden outside our house. The nightly revels and early morning concerts held on the turf, in defiance of the Garden Committee's rules, filled us with dismay. Old General O'Currie, who lives a few doors off, vowed and declared that the next time he was disturbed from his slumbers at 5 A.M. he would have recourse to the revolver which he always kept in his bedroom, 'and let fly into the whole d—— d lot of them, by Jove!'

But fate had ordained otherwise. Sandy's frailties were indeed avenged, but neither by poison nor pistol-shot. One unlucky day he disappeared. At first we made light of it, knowing at that time he was paying his attentions to a young and charming tabby at No. 25. But after forty-eight hours had elapsed we began to be uneasy. We sent round to all the adjacent houses to make inquiries after him, but without success. We had cards printed and dispatched by post to every shop and dwelling in the neighbourhood, offering a handsome reward for his recovery. Alas, all in vain! We never saw Sandy again. I hope he came to no harm—I mean no bodily injury. But he was a handsome and valuable cat, well worth stealing. And my belief has always been that he was carried off and sold to some dealer.

After the demise of Mr. Moss the household became inconsolable, and it was generally agreed that out of respect to his memory a reasonable time should elapse before any steps were taken to supply his place. An impression seemed to prevail, indeed, that the void occasioned by his loss in all our hearts was one which no four-footed pet could ever fill again. Phyllis, whose opinion on such a point no one ventured to question, vowed and declared that she could never love another dog as well as her lamented favourite, and, in short, we came to regard any suggestion to the contrary as unfeeling and heartless.

Time, however, will fortunately assuage the bitterest of domestic griefs, and when, after a trip to Switzerland, we had all returned in good health and spirits, I watched my opportunity and made a secret expedition to the neighbourhood of Seven Dials, with the view of inspecting the stock of several eminent dog-fanciers in that region. The result was that one fine October morning there arrived at our house a cab, out of which briskly stepped a stout and rather shrewd-looking gentleman in a velveteen coat, fur cap, and corduroy trousers, carrying a Yorkshire toy terrier in his hand, with two others peering out of his coat pockets, while a couple more followed at his heels at the imminent risk of being trodden on, as he wiped his feet at the door mat.

Presently they all came bounding into the dining-room, whence (their manners being as yet undisciplined and free from all sense of propriety) they were speedily allowed to escape from a window into the adjoining garden, where we inspected them and held a brief consultation as to their respective merits.

To choose one out of five puppies, all presenting various physical attractions of form and colour, and asserting their individual claims to attention by barking in a chorus, would under ordinary circumstances have been no easy matter, but as it luckily turned out three of this happy family were sisters, and as their sex placed them by general consent *hors de concours*, the choice lay between their two long-haired brothers, brown and grey. Our destinies in this world, whether we pass through it on two or four legs, are often ruled by trifles. While we were still deliberating, the gentleman in velveteen remarked 'that colour was in course a matter of taste, some parties inclining to brown while others preferred silver-grey, but that if we wanted a lively and reg'lar good-tempered little chap, with a good 'ead and lots of spring in him, we couldn't do better than take "Tiny."'

On hearing his name the brown puppy gave such a vigorous jump into the air, that he had some difficulty to alight on his feet again. This decided us. The gentleman in velveteen withdrew after pocketing two of the terriers and carrying the others. Tiny made a pathetic but unsuccessful bolt after him as the door closed, but thenceforth became our property. He had been represented by a sort of poetical—or perhaps I should say a dog-fanciful—license, as sixteen months old and free from distemper, and before remitting a cheque to his master, I asked whether he would mind sending me a memorandum to that effect. In due course I received the following reply :—

Monday.

Dear Sir—The lowest price of the Dog is what my man told you and verey cheape he has a cold in one eye I carnt tell you how long it will be or how it may turn out dogs has so meney things come on them now to what they used to have that I never give a Warranted with heney live Stock.

Yours Obd. Sert.,

JOE BARKER.

After a little training in deportment and the conventional usages of society, Tiny became a general favourite. He was, it must be confessed, distinguished by no accomplishments, and indeed the only trick he ever learned was to jump over a stick held about three inches from the ground when a biscuit was placed on the other side of it. His early but deep-rooted aversion to children's stockings, manifested by an unfortunate tendency to snap at them whenever he got a chance, landed us in some difficulties, especially on one occasion, when an indignant mother, accompanied by a policeman, presented herself at our door, and insisted on having the dog immediately slaughtered as a preliminary step towards bringing an action for damages. But faithful Phyllis, taking possession of her new pet, bade defiance to the law, and the honest constable after a careful survey of the infant's calves declared that he could find no mark of injury upon them. A huge slice of cake for the child and a profound apology to his mamma brought this unlucky affair to a happy issue.

Ladies' pocket handkerchiefs, the legs of male visitors' trousers, and the corners of housemaids' aprons afterwards became in turn the objects of Tiny's marked, not to say misdirected, attention; but no serious harm ensued, and everyone said it was only his play

He was a pretty little dog, with an unfailing appetite, but careful in his diet. He wisely abstained from rich food. Cold roast mutton was his favourite dish, and the less bread he had with it the better he was pleased, but of spinach, perhaps on sanitary grounds, he always partook freely.

As he grew older his long brown hair became tinged with silver, and having a remarkably pretty head his portrait was painted, and presented as a birthday gift to his fond mistress by a generous friend. How the restless little being was induced to remain quiet long enough for the completion of the picture has always been a marvel to me. Whether he came to a confidential understanding with the lady artist on the subject of biscuits, or whether, as I rather believe, she had acquired through long experience the knack of humouring her sitters, I don't know, but certain it is that in due course the portrait was finished, and was pronounced by everyone to be a capital likeness.

Tiny was very regular and methodical in his habits, and divided his time in certain proportions between the various rooms of the house and the garden. Having once established a certain routine, he adhered to it with great precision. For instance, on his master's return home every evening, after greeting him in the entrance hall, Tiny would run before him into the study, look up wistfully towards the door of a certain cabinet, and bark energetically until a duster was taken out. Seizing one corner of this, while his master held the other, Tiny would enter with great zeal into a brief game of 'pull devil, pull baker,' and make believe by sheer force of superior strength to tug his human play-mate into the adjoining room. If this fiction was faithfully preserved up to the end of the struggle, the little creature would rush off with a triumphant air, wagging his tail. But if by any accident the game was abandoned before its climax, he at once became disconcerted, like a child baulked in his play.

I don't think he liked being combed and brushed every morning, but after being accustomed to that ordeal he submitted to it with resignation, partly from his respect for routine, and partly I believe because he came to regard it at last in the light of a religious exercise.

Tiny never grew fat or unwieldy, and indeed he was not naturally a greedy dog. It was therefore no doubt from a mistaken idea about proprietary rights that he returned to his platter and hastily bolted the remnants of his dinner whenever Belshazzar (the cat) entered the room at meal time. His sense of humour was remarkable, and manifested itself in various ways. But his favourite joke was to get up an imaginary 'row' with his master, to whom he was greatly attached. Anything served as a pretext for the dispute, and the more trifling it was the better the fun. The assurance which the little creature showed in his mimic wrath was wonderful. Nothing daunted him. It was in vain that he was scolded and threatened with a walking-stick. He only barked the louder and wagged his tail more vigorously. Sometimes, when both combatants were exhausted, a truce was made, and then to see Tiny rush up and lick his master's hand with delight was truly pathetic.

Tiny was often on the sick list. Rheumatism, coughs, boils, and toothache attacked him in turn, but, thanks to the careful nursing of his devoted Phyllis, he pulled through these disorders, and considering the amount of extra petting, not to mention warm blankets and tit-bits, which he got during convalescence, I think he rather enjoyed being laid up.

One very severe winter, when he imprudently ventured in the snow without his sealskin coat, he caught a severe cold which resulted in chronic bronchitis. We were all in despair. Every veterinary surgeon of note at the West End was consulted on the case ; one eminent practitioner actually arrived at the house in his brougham. Draughts, pills, embrocations, and what not, were prescribed for him. I am almost ashamed to remember what I paid for medicine and attendance. But the cough went on, poor Tiny got thinner and thinner, and we began to think that 'physicians were in vain.'

What could we expect? they all asked. The dog was eleven years old and his days were numbered. Autumn came and we went for a six weeks' trip on the Continent, secretly doubting, though we dared not say so, whether we should ever see Tiny again. But while we were away, it occurred to the faithful

Phyllis that change of air would do him good. She took him to her country home, where he was made free of the garden and adjoining meadows. He ran about, made friends with the family cat, rose early, hunted imaginary rabbits, and thoroughly enjoyed himself. Better still, he got rid of his cough, and when we came back from abroad we found him thoroughly convalescent, and as lively as any middle-aged terrier could expect to be.

He reached the ripe age of fifteen, and though rather 'groggy on his pins,' long remained in capital condition and enjoyed a romp with his master as much as ever. He succumbed, however, at last to time. The morning bath—once a weekly ceremony—was on account of his advancing years less frequently prescribed, but for obvious reasons it could not be altogether given up. One day he had just been placed in his little tub of comfortably warm water, and Phyllis was standing ready with a hot towel, when he just 'heeled over' as the sailors say, and was gone in a moment, poor little dog!

. . . . . .

He was buried in the back garden, his faithful nurse Phyllis attending the funeral with streaming eyes. Indeed, we were all greatly distressed at his demise. But it is a comfort to think that he had had a life of almost uninterrupted happiness.

His successor is called 'Pixie,' a name borrowed from the fairy lore of Devonshire, but to which he has no sort of local right, being a native of Leeds, and a small rough-haired terrier of Yorkshire breed. He travelled up to London in a soap-box about nine inches square, and seems to have resented the indignity by a rooted dislike to brown windsor ever since. He is full grown now, weighs about seven pounds, and is of undaunted courage. I never yet saw him attack a German boar-hound, and I trust for his sake that he never may. But he is quite capable of doing so, and the probable result of such an encounter would never occur to him. There never was such a cheeky little animal. He has differences with other dogs about twice his size, and is quite indignant at being rescued. He runs after formidable-looking rams in the Park, and I believe he would 'chivvy' a hippopotamus if he had a chance. The family cat (a huge and good-natured creature) could slaughter him at a moment's notice, but is content to fly before Pixie, who teases him dreadfully, craftily waiting for him in dark corners, pulling his fine Persian tail, bowling him over and rolling on him out of pure mischief, until poor pussy is fain to take refuge on the mantelpiece. Even big collie-dogs and retrievers do not resent his impertinence, but open their big mouths with a wondering smile as he barks at them, wag their tails and trot amiably away.

The fact is that Pixie is a general favourite, and makes friends with all his companions whether they stand on two or four legs. For all his warlike demonstrations he is the most affectionate little soul in the world, and it is impossible to help loving him. As for his accomplishments, he can fetch and carry; beg for biscuits in the most approved fashion; find his pet india-rubber ball when it is hidden; jump over a stick and through a hoop a dozen times running for a lump of sugar; while for peeling hot chestnuts without burning himself I don't know his equal. His coat gets longer and more silvery every day; his eyes are full of fun; his ears, which happily have never been clipped in accordance with the barbarous custom of former days, are pricked with a knowing air, and, though his tail was reduced in early life to modest proportions, he carries what remains of it gaily.

He welcomes all visitors enthusiastically, recognising all old friends with marked cordiality and doing his best to conciliate new ones, especially those who have well-polished boots, the flavour of Day and Martin's blacking having a peculiar charm for his palate which seems irresistible. He has learnt to distinguish the postman's knock from the rat-a-tat-tat of Mr. James Yellowplush, and both from the monosyllabic rap given at the street-door by tradesmen's boys, whom he regards with uneasiness—not to say aversion.

His notion of supreme bliss is a run in Kensington Gardens without his leather 'leader,' which he regards as a ridiculous invention, wholly inconsistent with the liberties of the subject and a proper sense of canine dignity. He is devoted to children, and evidently considers their games in the Park as having been organised for his special amusement. He runs after the balls which they throw at each other and carries them off in triumph. He tries to persuade little boys that hoops were made to jump through, and that it is a waste of energy to trundle them. He 'fields' on his own account during improvised cricket, hangs on by the tails of toy-horses as if they were his natural prey, and once nearly frightened an infant out of its wits by leaping into a perambulator with the object of purloining its rattle. He respects his collar and bells as a badge of office, but, though a dog of taste, he seems absolutely indifferent to the colour of the ribbon top-knot which forms its crowning glory. I rather think he prefers pale yellow because it reminds him of bones, but I am not sure.

Pixie is of very active habits and takes a vast deal of exercise during the day. Even in wet weather he devotes himself to athletics and, *faute de mieux*, will run up and down stairs by way of a 'constitutional.' In the evening he lies by the drawing-room fire planning new romps for to-morrow. He is very punctual in his habits, and obeys the sound of the dinner bell with great alacrity.

It need scarcely be said that Phyllis, though by no means forgetful of her dear departed pets, has transferred her affection to the latest favourite. She feeds him, doctors him, gives him his weekly bath—an honour which I firmly believe he would accept from no other hands—caresses him, lectures him when he allows his sense of humour to carry him beyond the bounds of propriety, and shares her little dormitory with him, where he sleeps on a cosy rug by the side of her bed.

It would be invidious to gauge the scale of his affection as manifested to various members of the household—but I do not hesitate to say that he gives the preference to ladies—partly, perhaps, on the *place aux dames* principle, but mainly, I think, because he finds their laps more conducive to repose than the trousered legs of his male friends. For a prolonged siesta, however, he wisely contents himself with a soft cushion on the best arm-chair, and in the absence of human companions he makes himself quite happy with pussy.

Tim is older and wiser than Pixie, but, like all

sensible creatures who have attained middle life, he regards the frivolities of youth with a calm and indulgent benevolence. It is almost a moral lesson to see that big, solemn, stately cat, robed in fur of the finest quality, decorated with martial whiskers and a huge fluffy tail, condescending to play at hide and seek or pretending to fly in alarm round the table in order to indulge Pixie in the pleasures of the chase. But he knows where to draw the line, and when he is tired of romping he withdraws behind the mantelpiece curtain, tucks it well around his portly form, and, thus secured from his beloved pal and tormenter, enjoys the warmth of the fire and sleeps in peace.

I am very fond of children's society—that is for half an hour or so—and I am told that it is endurable (some say enjoyable) for a longer period. But there is no nursery in 'Terra-cottage,' and when this is the case you may be sure that four-footed pets have it all their own way.

When men and women don't care for small animals, depend on it it is due to one of three causes. Either their education has been neglected, in which case they are much to be pitied—or they have children who absorb all their love, in which case it is to be hoped that they will not be disillusioned—or they are of an unsympathetic nature altogether, in which case there is nothing more to be said.

But I can't fancy a truly happy home without pets of some kind, and if it is a fact—as it most undoubtedly is—that many of the wisest and best of mankind have found pleasant companionship, amusement, fidelity, and affection in what is called the lower scale of creation, who shall blame more ordinary mortals, like you and me, dear madam, for yielding to the same weakness and sharing the same joy?

CHAPTER V

MY BOOKS

When we first entered into possession of our house, a great debate ensued as to what would be the fittest name for the little sitting-room which I chiefly occupy myself, and which I like to consider specially my own. As it contains the greater part of my books, my wife, who has a strong sense of dignity in all domestic matters, proposed that it should be known as 'The Library,' and there is certainly a mansion-like sound in the word which prepossesses strangers. On the other hand, Cousin Bridget, who in my absence covers my writing desk with her dictionaries, grammars, and exercise books in profusion, suggested that 'The Study' would be a far more appropriate title.

Now, I frequently read and write in the place, but as I generally enjoy a pipe there late in the evening, I thought, being an unpretentious sort of man, that it would answer all practical purposes if we called it 'The Smoking Room.' That proposal having been overruled, as savouring too much of dissolute and bachelor habits, we adopted 'The Sanctum' as a compromise, and this does very well—the only drawback being that new servants, until undeceived on the point, have a tendency to conceive that it is used as a private chapel, and expect to be summoned there for family prayers.

My collection of books is not a large one. It comprises, perhaps, five hundred volumes all told, and they are a very mixed lot. In a big library, of course it is possible to classify and arrange works under special heads; history, travel, fiction, poetry, and so forth. But on the shelves of my sanctum it is a question not so much of subject as of size—quarto volumes are ranged with quartos, no matter what they respectively contain, and octavos go alongside of each other, be their pages grave or gay. It is a sort of literary republic. Some are smartly bound in 'tree calf' and green morocco, others in 'tooled antique,' others in humble cloth, but there is no distinction of rank—all are housed alike in good oak bookcases, with no distinction but that of shape.

This heterogeneous arrangement rather suits my temperament, for, to say the truth, I am what is called a desultory reader. I have an idle habit of taking down a book at random according to the humour I am in. Sometimes I feel inclined for Macaulay and am presently absorbed in one of his brilliant essays, clear and precise in language, sparkling with humour, and distinguished by that logical method of criticism which seems to carry conviction with it. History as illustrated by his magic pen is no dry record of government statecraft and international strife. It becomes as interesting as any novel.

I know it is the fashion nowadays to say there was too much romance about it. Perhaps his political bias led him occasionally to overstate a case, to misinterpret the motives of those whom he disliked, and eulogise some of his heroes to an extent which they did not deserve. But, after all, what chronicler, from the Venerable Bede to Mr. Freeman, can escape this imputation? Even contemporary writers on science, art, and philosophy are always contradicting each other. Who is to judge between them? *Scribimus indocti doctique.* And we, the great majority of unlearned ones, who are unable to decide when experts disagree, cannot wait for the verdict of posterity. We must choose for ourselves. Macaulay may not be infallible, but his books delight me nevertheless.

Partly from old associations, and partly because I am too lazy to glean from the mass of information collated by later writers, I can spend an hour or two very pleasantly over a volume of Hume and Smollett. Their entertaining work is not much in request among enlightened students of the present day, but I have no time to consult Eadmer and

Boniface, Matthew Pain and Roger of Wendover. I am irritated when I find the names of my old friends Canute and Egbert spelt Cnut and Ecgbehrt. Who knows what the 'thegn' of Cawdor means? I like to talk still of the battle of *Hastings*. The victory at *Senlac* seems to me quite another thing. I know that I ought to read Stubbs, Ellis, Kemble, Morley, and other authorities. Yet somehow I don't.

After all, most of us who are not erudite scholars must take our history second-hand. Fifty years hence it will not much matter what notions I have formed respecting the characters of Mary Queen of Scots, Oliver Cromwell, and William III. Indeed, if I adopted the views of certain contemporary historians they would be somewhat conflicting. *Faute de mieux*, Hume and Smollett will serve my purpose.

The appetite for ancient lore is robust with some readers. They can partake of the solid food provided for them by Gibbon, Hallam and Grote. Others cannot digest it easily. They like daintier and more appetising dishes—seasoned with a little romance or records of domestic life—such as those served up by Sir Walter Scott, or that good old gossip Samuel Pepys, whose famous Diary gives one a better picture of life in the 17th century than many a learned treatise.

The late Professor Brewer's indefatigable researches

respecting the reign of Henry VIII. represent a monument of human industry, which we must all reverence, but if, without following in his footsteps, one wants a little insight into the life and times of 'bluff King Hal,' Mr. Ernest Law's delightful 'History of Hampton Court' will supply it.

I won't pretend that I have read steadily through my twelve volumes of Sismondi, though they deal with a country which, next to my own, I love best in the world, but there they are, bound in gilt Roman parchment, on my shelves ready for reference and enlightenment on a hundred matters about which it is well to refresh one's memory before a visit to the sunny south.

As for J. Addington Symonds's 'History of the Italian Renaissance'—a bulky work, too, in its way—you may be sure that has a place of honour in my little library. What a mass of information on art, literature, poetry, romance, and politics is contained in those seven scholarly books! What patient research, cultivated taste, and judicious criticism they represent! For style of diction, intimate acquaintance with his subject, and wide range of study, the author has scarcely a rival.

It is a pity that one has not time and energy to read more, but it is sadder still for some of us to reflect how soon what one reads is forgotten. My memory is like a sieve. General impressions of a great man's character, leading events in history, turning points in the destiny of nations, these linger—some of them are fixed indelibly in one's mind. But details, dates of battles, names of second-rate heroes, statesmen, geographical boundaries, periods of national prosperity or influence, all the useful minutiæ which help to build up knowledge, and tend to make what Bacon calls a 'full man,' are provokingly evanescent.

To have a retentive brain is surely one of the indispensable conditions to success in life. I take up a volume of Gibbons's 'Decline and Fall,' and am amazed at the huge accumulation of mere facts which he must have sought out and collated as a foundation for that prodigious work. Every page teems with notes or quotations from ancient writers—Cicero, Strabo, Pliny, Tacitus, Philostratus, Eusebius—a hundred names would not complete the list. One's brain reels under the contemplation of such labour. A single chapter in the book would suffice to make a man's reputation as a scholar. You read on and on, admiring the author's industry, his vast command of language, his perspicuity, his wit and covert satire. But when you have come to the end (and even the 'Decline and Fall' has a *finis*) how much do you recollect of details?

Supposing you were asked a month later by some earnest inquirer to give him some particulars of the siege of Aquileia, or the battles of Cibalis and Mardia. Could you tell him what led to the revolt of Procopius? Who were the White Huns of Sogdiana? When did Gregory Nazianzen accept the mission to Constantinople? Do you recollect anything at all of the life and character of Stilicho?

Alas! I greatly fear that most of these matters, deeply interesting to you when you read about them, will have filtered away into oblivion within a fortnight afterwards. What *memoria technica* will help you in such a case? Some semi-historical works, indeed, from the very nature of their aim and the author's ingenious method, bear intellectual fruit of which the flavour lingers long after it has been consumed. It is not the facts adduced in support of this or that theory, but the theory itself, which leaves a lasting impression.

Among such books I think Lecky's 'European Morals' and 'History of Rationalism' may fairly be reckoned. They deal with questions which, to the end of time, cannot fail to interest every thoughtful reader. Unsettling, perhaps, in some respects; rending veils which the timid have not cared to peep behind; subversive of some fond delusions; illumining dark corners which do not quite bear the light, and explaining a ay much that one learnt in childhood to love and revere, but written in no scoffing or cynical strain. The truth must be told, but our philosopher tells it gently—I fancy sometimes with a sort of kindly sympathy for the painful doubt which his revelations create. In one passage, I remember, he dwells rather sadly on the fact that an increase of knowledge is not always attended by a commensurate increase of happiness. Better sometimes to be simple and ignorant than learn that which sooner or later must cut us adrift from early faith!

Darwin is another benevolent reformer. He never dogmatises. In reading his 'Origin of Species' and 'Descent of Man,' one is struck with the singular modesty with which his views are expressed, or rather suggested. The scientific facts to which he draws attention are, for the most part, now regarded as indisputable. But he allows you to draw your own inference.

It is curious to remember what alarm was occasioned among many good folks a score of years ago when the theory of Evolution first took a definite form—just such another panic as, I suppose, was raised when Galileo asserted that the earth moved round the sun, or when the geologists discovered that the age of the world had been underrated at 4,000 years. 400,000 will not suffice for them now. Yet it is not uncommon to find converts to Darwinism even among the clergy.

'Sic volvenda ætas commutat tempora rerum,
Quod fuit in pretio fit nullo denique honore;
Porro aliud succedit et e contemptibus exit,'
&c. &c.

For my own part I confess myself a dunce in science. But, looking on the question from a social point of view, evolution does not strike me as such a terrible heresy. After all, it is more cheerful to trace man's life back to an anthropoid ape than to contemplate its extinction by bacilli.

Beyond an odd volume or two on zoology and a few elementary works on physics, I fear that my library does not afford much evidence of scientific culture. If I come across subjects of this class in the ordinary course of reading and want to be enlightened I turn to that invaluable repository of useful knowledge, Chambers' Encyclopædia, and clear up my doubts in five minutes. I remember with a feeling akin to remorse the large sums of money which were spent on my education. But I am consoled when I find in later life how much instruction can be obtained for the modest outlay of five pounds.

If I were consulted by a young householder of limited means as to the formation of a small library I should say: 'Begin with books of reference.' Encyclopædias, biographical dictionaries, chronological records, scientific primers, and other works of a compendious form do not, of course, satisfy the specialist, but they supply a good basis for wider and deeper information to the average reader, and, thanks to the days in which we live, are within the reach of most purses.

It is true that the Bard of Twickenham (who lived and died long before the Society for the Diffusion of Useful Knowledge was even dreamt of) cautions us to 'drink deep or taste not the Pierian spring,' but in this modern work-a-day world only people who can command exceptional leisure or exceptional energy find leisure to 'drink deep,' and even a superficia acquaintance with some subjects is better than stark ignorance.

'Beware of handbook knowledge!' cries Mr. Ruskin, but what would the nineteenth century traveller do, whether he migrates on the Continent or wanders in his native land, without that little red octavo volume which is the *vade mecum* of every British tourist? I have at least a dozen of Murray's famous guides on my shelves and can truly say that they have materially enhanced the pleasures of many a holiday trip both at home and abroad.

'Annuals' have long since gone out of fashion Indeed, the very name, as applied to periodical literature, would seem unintelligible to the rising generation, who can choose from a dozen sixpenny magazines every month, and find in them far better illustrations and often better reading than could have been bought for a guinea in the early part of Queen Victoria's reign.

Yet there was a good deal to be learnt, too, from some of those old-world publications. I well remember the absorbing interest with which as a boy I conned over Hone's delightful volumes—'The Year Book,' 'The Table Book,' and 'The Everyday Book.' I have them still in a reprint, and I look with wonder at the queer, rudely-executed wood-cuts scattered through their pages, more like caricatures by Cruikshank than serious illustrations. But in the text one finds a good deal of information about old English customs, local traditions, provincial ceremonies, Church festivals, and popular lore collated in a useful form.

A special old favourite of mine is Burton's 'Anatomy of Melancholy.' Dr. Johnson used to say that it was the only book which took him out of bed two hours sooner than he wished to rise. It has often kept me up two hours after I have bidden everyone goodnight! Was ever so much erudition, so much world-wisdom, so much quaint advice, such a rich variety of entertainment, comprised in one volume? It has been aptly described as 'the delight of the learned, the solace of the indolent, the refuge of the uninformed.' In its own day it went through three editions. To how many generations of readers has it since afforded pleasure and instruction? Just as the Coliseum at Rome became a sort of quarry for the Renaissance builders, so Burton's 'Anatomy' has been ruthlessly pillaged by later writers. The author of 'Tristram Shandy' plagiarised whole passages from its pages. Milton is said to have based a well known poem on its philosophy. Literary critics complain that the book is too full of quotations, but I suspect that a good many nameless scribblers have been glad to use them second hand.

It is perhaps to be regretted that amid the crowd of passages cited from ancient and mediæval literature the author should have told us so little of himself and his own sentiments. But no one can read his analysis of the causes of melancholy—idleness, physical influences, ambition, over-study, love, poverty, ambition, covetousness, and jealousy—without feeling that Burton was an enemy of superstition, impatient of hypocrisy, intolerant of vice, an advocate of manly pleasures and exercise, and a hater of prigs and grumblers. What could one say in higher praise of most men?

It is probably true that the compilation of his stupendous 'monograph' did not relieve him of his spleen. Indeed, I doubt whether the preparation of manuscript in any form is conducive to that result. But he has left to posterity a work which will be prized wherever the English language is read or spoken. One can scarcely imagine any library complete without it.

I cannot afford rare and choice editions of old books, but some years ago I picked up a capital copy of the 'Spectator,' published in sixteen small octavo volumes while George I. was still on the throne. It is printed in bold type, with the pretty initial letters, head lines, and tail pieces which were in vogue at that period, and which lend a picturesque interest to the text.

I don't suppose that any one of our own time ever got through the whole of it. Life is too short and books are too numerous for the task. But I like to take down an odd volume now and then, and conjure up visions of life in the early part of the last century—a queer complex kind of life—half naïve, half artificial, distinguished by sentiments of the highest order, and social habits perhaps not quite so elevated. I love to read Addison's sermons on the vanity of human ambition, though he did choose an Earl's widow for his wife, and Sir Richard Steele's moral precepts, though I know he did not act up to them.

It is pleasant to imagine oneself in the company of a model country gentleman, Sir Roger de Coverley, and that charming old beau Will Honeycomb; to find the fleeting follies of the day so graphically described, so amiably satirised. As we turn over page after page pictures of old London and the haunts of the 'quality' pass before us, as though in a diorama. We see the dandies bewigged and powdered in Hyde Park, the lady gossips gathered round Mrs. Modish's tea-table. We are at the Opera House and hear the pit joining in the chorus on the stage. We make acquaintance with Lesbia, Sophronia, and Lady Fanny Fickle, adorned with patches, encircled by hoops, and equipped with fans. These memorable essays—some serious, others trivial, but most of them interesting, must have been a fresh source of weekly pleasure in countless homes for a period of four years.

They are delightful reading now, although nearly two centuries old. The modern purist may find in them a coarse expression here and there, characteristic of days when a spade was called a spade, but nothing that is intentionally vicious or corrupt.

There is, I fear, but little romance in my nature. It is certain that I have not much taste for modern poetry. The most exalted sentiments embodied in nineteenth century verse do not stir me to emotion. I often agree with a great deal which the author has to say, but I do not see what occasion there is for singing it. I know that my views on this point are crude and heretical, but I cannot help it.

The serious versification of sentiment nowadays seems to me almost unreal and affected. I have read

Tennyson's works with pleasure, Swinburne's 'Chastelard' and 'Atalanta in Calydon,' W. Morris's 'Earthly Paradise,' and a few of Alfred Austin's pieces. I have tried to read Browning, but my taste, as I have said, does not lie in the direction of recent rhyme. The world seems to me to have outgrown the necessity for this form of literary art. Such is my strange obtuseness!

It is very different with the old poets. I can enjoy Chaucer, notwithstanding the initial difficulty of mastering mediæval English. I know my 'Canterbury Tales' and the 'Romaunt of the Rose' pretty well, and though those famous works, for obvious reasons, cannot be recommended for general reading, sooner or later they must be studied by every man who aims at even a superficial acquaintance with English literature. A healthy love of nature, a keen sense of the picturesque, a graphic power of narration, a chivalrous reverence for virtue, a loyalty to ancient faith, and thorough knowledge of human character in all its aspects, may be traced in many a page, and combine to enhance our admiration for the father of English poetry.

I cannot pretend to an equal enthusiasm for Dryden. His versions of the classics are indeed wonderful achievements, not on account of their accuracy—for who can really *translate* poetry?—but because of the zest with which he threw himself into the task, imbibing as it were the very spirit of his great originals. He is as bitter as Juvenal, as erotic as Ovid, as stately as Virgil.

Pagan life and mythology are revived and realised by the 17th century poet. The gods and heroes of antiquity converse familiarly in our mother tongue. Æneas and Dido are no longer the creatures of fiction, but human beings. The follies and vices of ancient Rome are as graphically described as if the narrator were lashing the libertines and demireps of the Restoration. The author gives full license to his pen, and writes of many naughty matters with a certain gusto, as if he really enjoyed the task. But when we turn from the 'Satires' and the 'Art of Love,' and find the man who could draw upon the English language for such very free versions of those racy works, posing as a pillar of the Church and defender of the Faith in the 'Hind and the Panther,' it is the poet rather than the controversialist whom we admire.

Whatever our theological convictions may be—Roman Catholic, Anglican, or Calvinist, one may, I think, distrust the sincerity of such a champion, and feel that here at least Dryden was out of his element.

The old heroic metre has been so long out of fashion, and English poetry from the days of Byron down to our own time has assumed so many different forms, that it would be difficult to find among the admirers of Tennyson and Swinburne many who take much genuine pleasure in Pope's works. Yet not a century ago the 'Rape of the Lock' was read by thousands, who pronounced it one of the finest poems in our language, and who turned from the 'Lay of the last Minstrel' as the feeble production of a degenerate age.

For my own part I confess to be old fashioned in my literary tastes. In spite of the monotonous, one might say perfunctory, character of its versification, and although much of its interest depends upon contemporary events and squabbles which the world has long forgotten, I can read the 'Dunciad' with sincere enjoyment. The brilliant wit, the lofty scorn, the majestic rhythm of that memorable satire, compel the reader's attention and make one almost share the author's wrath.

As for the 'Essay on Man,' though some of the sentiments which it embodies may appear trite to deeply read students of philosophy, it seems to my half tutored mind one of the noblest and most thoughtful compositions ever penned. The narrow creed in which the poet had been brought up, the artificial and often vicious character of the society in which he lived, the educational disadvantages under which he suffered, to say nothing of his physical infirmities, only enhance one's admiration for the wonderful courage and genius which inspired his pen. Every line is pregnant with meaning. Not a word is wasted. The polished elegance of the verse is almost unrivalled. In that broad, calm survey of human nature, we find reflected the most advanced and liberal thoughts of the author's own time, and an almost prophetic insight into theories which the progress of science and the gradual extinction of prejudice have since evolved.

It would be a curious and interesting subject for inquiry by our modern advocates for 'higher' culture how far their doctrines have tended to increase the study of Shakespeare. Young folks nowadays flock to see Mr. Irving's revivals at the Lyceum. The scenery, the costumes, the mounting, the artistic beauty and scrupulous attention to realism in those famous representations, to say nothing of fashion's influence, cannot fail to make them attractive. But out of every hundred spectators among the nightly audience, how many are familiar with the text of the great playwright?

I have a notion that a genuine love of Shakespeare must be acquired in early youth. In my own case I remember that although slow at construing Euripides, at the age of fifteen I knew by heart whole passages in 'Hamlet,' 'Macbeth,' 'The Merchant of Venice, and several other plays. To this day I have never forgotten them. Is there any period of one's life, indeed, from youth to old age, in which those immortal pages are not enjoyable? The wide scope and comprehensive humanity of the genius which inspires them, the versatile nature of its aim, the varied direction of its sympathy, ought surely to win all hearts.

When Nasmyth invented his huge but docile hammer, the world was lost in admiration of the great engine which could drive a pile or crack a filbert. Shakespeare's vast but delicately poised intellect possessed this kind of power. There is nothing too high and nothing too lowly for him. Friendship, love, wrath, ambition, mirth, jealousy, courage, pusillanimity, and avarice, every passion which ennobles and every sin which degrades mankind, he could analyse and describe.

But the great philosopher was neither pedant nor ascetic. He knew the world in all its phases. In his finest tragedies he is tempted now and then to introduce a spice of humour. His romance, as we know, is often mingled with burlesque. Here is the high-souled Prince of Denmark puzzling over the great problem of existence, and presently appear a couple of grave-diggers chaffing each other over their gruesome task.

Again, how easily the most versatile of authors passes from the lofty utterances of Henry IV. to the jocund bluster of Falstaff. He is equally at home whether consorting with courtiers in the king's presence chamber or hobnobbing with Bardolph in the ale-house. Even on the eve of Cleopatra's death, after we have been listening to Mark Antony and Cæsar, the yokel who brings her the asp must have his little joke about 'the worm.'

Who but Shakespeare would have dared, in a play of which the scene is laid in Greece with a Theseus, a Lysander and Demetrius included in the *dramatis personæ*, to introduce an episode derived from fairy lore and such an ignominious personage as Bottom? With the forest of Ardennes for a background, and in the midst of all the romantic love of sylvan life which some of the scenes inspire, we are in turn saddened by the melancholy reflections of Jacques, and moved to laughter by honest Touchstone.

Mr. Ruskin says somewhere, 'How marvellously since Shakespeare's time have we lost the faculty of being amused by bad puns!' But after making due allowance for change of time and the conditions of social life, was there ever such a funny picture of Bumbledom as that presented by Dogberry and Verges? A sixteenth century Boz might have written it, but then a sixteenth century Boz could not have invented Othello. Think of the sublime passages in Richard III., the horrible invective of Timon, and then remember that the humour of Christopher Sly and the roguish songs of Autolycus were all derived from one and the same source! It is simply marvellous. Shades of Collier, Drake, Johnson, Malone, Lamb, and Schlegel, explain it if you can?

Among the books in my library which I am always wanting leisure to read through from beginning to end are two bulky volumes containing Swift's 'Life and Works.' At present I have barely accomplished a third of the task, which is perhaps as much as can be expected from the average of casual and pre-occupied students; yet the biography of the great satirist is in itself of such absorbing interest that no romance in the English language, no chapter of English history, could be more attractive. His early trials and poverty, his turbulent youth, the ignominious service which fate obliged him to enter, but which must have filled his soul with wrath, the gradual triumph of his transcendent genius, his political influence and relations with the great world, the mystery of his loves and friendship, the dark and melancholy cloud which closed and overshadowed his eventful and brilliant career, combine to enlist our sympathies and perpetuate the memory of Swift among many of us who have never read the 'Drapier's Letters' and to whom the 'Tale of a Tub' is almost unintelligible.

But for those superficial readers who love a bit of old-world gossip, who wish to know something of the man, apart from the author and politician, with all his whims, his personal tastes and idiosyncrasies, what more delightful reading is there than the 'Journal to Stella'? Posterity owes to that unfortunate lady a deep debt of gratitude for having preserved a series of letters richer in detail and more varied in entertainment than were perhaps ever set up in type or will ever pass through the post again. In the whole range of English literature and published correspondence there is nothing like them.

As for the 'Travels of Mr. Lemuel Gulliver,' I had read them all through at the age of ten, in the well-known edition illustrated by Grandville, the first notable birthday gift which I ever received. At that early age it shared my childish interest with the 'Adventures of Robinson Crusoe' and the 'Arabian Nights' Entertainments.' The bitter sarcasm, the splendid mendacity of the author were only revealed to me in later years. Perhaps it is the sole work of fiction extant which for many generations past has fascinated readers from boyhood to mature age.

In some old-fashioned homes, illumined maybe by a reverence for Dr. Watts, and actuated no doubt by an honest desire to protect inexperienced youth from the baneful influence of risky reading, paterfamilias used to keep certain of his books under lock and key, lest they should be perused on some unlucky day by the juvenile inmates of his household. I have no secret cupboards in my sanctum, and I am not sure whether if I had I should devote them to such a purpose. There are volumes in every library which boys and girls had better leave alone, but injunctions to children on such a point would, I fear, be attended by the same result as those which Bluebeard gave to Fatima, and only create an irresistible curiosity for research.

For my own part I recognise in the dust which accumulates on my calf-bound copies of Wycherley, Congreve, Vanbrugh, and Farquhar, a pleasing evidence that the famous dramas of the Restoration are rarely opened by anyone but their lawful owner. They are not, it must be confessed, very edifying reading, and one thinks with a certain sense of shame of an age when such plays can have been deliberately written, rehearsed, enacted, and no doubt received with applause by an enthusiastic audience of all ranks in English society. But they are not all equally vicious, and most of them, as we know, are redeemed from degradation by brilliant dialogue and flashes of wit which sparkle forth from those too often soiled pages like the light of a glow-worm lying in the mire.

A domestic Index Expurgatorius of our day ought, I suppose, to include the works of Henry Fielding, and yet one knows that a few generations back 'Tom Jones' and 'Amelia' were commonly read by decent folks of both sexes in many a British home. Are we more moral, I wonder, or only more squeamish than our grandfathers? I learnt more wickedness in my first month at a public school than I did at a much later date by the perusal of both those ingenious romances. I confess to a certain interest in the 'Adventures of Joseph Andrews.' The vein of quiet satire which runs through the biography of Mr. Jonathan Wild amuses me. 'Amelia,' after making due allowance for the lax morality of the age in which it was written, and for the 'high falutin'' character of the sentiment which it embodies, is, as we know, a work of long confessed excellence.

Smollett's works stand on a different level. The adventures of 'Roderick Random' and 'Peregrine Pickle' are familiar to all students of light literature in the last century, and were read no doubt with interest by the author's contemporaries, but at the present day, even his most ardent admirers would probably find a great deal of what schoolboys call 'skip' in those famous romances. 'Humphrey Clinker' is amusing as a description of English social life and manners a hundred years ago. But the epistolary form of narrative amplified to such an extent becomes tiresome after a while, and though our grandfathers seemed to have laughed over Mrs. Bramble's homely letters and the bad spelling of Winifred Jenkins, they present a form of fun which has somehow lost its flavour to modern taste, just as Gillray's caricatures appear coarse and grotesque to eyes which have been accustomed to the sketches and more refined humour of Leech and Du Maurier.

Boswell's 'Life of Johnson' is a book about which I suppose even the most casual reader is supposed to know something. It is like a cask of good ale which is found in every well-regulated household. You can't drink the whole of it at once. Indeed, I doubt whether it can be safely recommended for daily consumption. But an occasional draught is palatable and refreshing I take down such books from time to time, read a chapter or two, and put them back again. It is an idle habit, I know. No earnest student of literature goes to work in this way. Perhaps I am a trifler. But it is better to pick up information thus than no t at all, and I enjoy it.

Occupying a conspicuous place on my book shelves are the complete works of Dickens and Thackeray, which from boyhood to middle age have afforded me, in common with countless thousands of readers, a vast store of entertainment for which I can never be sufficiently grateful. At different times of my life and in various circumstances—in sickness and in health, abroad or at home, after a hard day's toil and in supreme idleness, from first to last, I reckon that I have read nearly every volume.

Comparisons are sometimes drawn between these great masters of fiction, but to no purpose. You might as well discuss the respective merits of music and painting, of red and white roses, or champagne and Burgundy. The world is divided on these points, and always will be. It is a question of taste. The two authors have but little in common. They regard their art from different standpoints. Their aims are, perhaps, identical, but their respective methods are completely at variance.

Speaking generally, one might say with confidence that Thackeray appeals to a more cultivated class ot readers than his friend and rival. Yet you will find now and then well educated people who prefer Dickens, and he certainly has the advantage in tenfold popularity among the masses. 'Boz' had the start in my affections. I read 'Oliver Twist' when I was in a round jacket, and to this day I think it the best of his earlier productions—excepting, perhaps, 'The Old Curiosity Shop.' In both an exquisite sense of humour commingles strangely with tragedy or pathos, though it must be confessed that the sentiment with which these stories are sprinkled appears somewhat cheap, and it tries one's patience to read poor Nancy's measured utterances in blank-verse prose.

It is obvious that most of Dickens's earlier novels owe their charm and vitality to his close observation of detail, and his power of describing the comic side of humble life or the peculiarities of people who would be nobodies in what is called society. But in portraying the follies and frailties of the 'upper ten' his satire approaches the grotesque. He could caricature a gentleman, but he rarely drew one.

His skill in planning a plot was extraordinary, but the nature of his inventive power seems mainly dramatic. The chief incidents of his novels—early and late, the *personnel* of his villains—the general action and conduct of his puppets—and even their conversation, were of the stage, stagey. He could never altogether get away from the footlights. I think he reached his culminating excellence in 'David Copperfield.' His latest works are not much to my taste. Their character is artificial and unlike himself. Perhaps the best of them is the 'Tale of Two Cities.'

The essence of Dickens's humour was indeed original, but in the more serious passages of his works the phraseology which he employed was largely influenced by the literary style of the day, and it was a deplorably pedantic style. Thackeray was the first to break away from it. He could not tolerate or adopt the stilted diction and utterly unreal colloquy which until he began to write, even the best novelists of his day put into the mouths of their heroes and heroines. The beings created by his active and ever fertile brain, from Colonel Newcome down to Harry Foker, talk like ordinary mortals, and when the author himself interrupts his narrative—as he frequently does—to chat with his readers, or point a moral from his story, it is in the easy language of a confidential friend.

This happy familiarity of style, combined as it was with an accurate and scholarlike knowledge of his mother tongue, a dexterous choice of words and a wonderfully subtle wit, constitutes to my mind the chief excellence of his literary mode, and marks it unmistakably as his own. It invests his fiction with an impression of reality which, so far as I can judge, was never conveyed by any other writer of our time. One thinks of the people whom he described not as mere types of character, but as actual men and women.

Thackeray is often spoken of, by readers who don't understand him, as a cynic—and nothing else; as an author who took a warped and perverted view of human nature; as a sceptic in morality, and so forth. Good heavens! Why, there are passages in 'Pendennis,' in 'Vanity Fair,' and the 'Newcomes' which could only have been written by a man with the highest sense of honour, of reverence for virtue, of sympathy with genuine sorrow and human weakness.

The range of his ability was wonderful. When he chose to put on the cap and bells his fooling was excellent. One can scarcely believe that the same man whose knowledge of history qualified him to deliver those brilliant lectures on the 'Four Georges,' and whose taste in art and literature found expression in some of the best essays of his time, could descend to such trivialities as 'The Adventures of Major Gahagan,' 'The Yellowplush Papers,' and 'Mrs. Perkins's Ball.' Yet for downright boyish fun there is nothing like them.

His sentiment seems all the more genuine because it is never strained or unduly accentuated. It is uttered in the simplest language, and with unconscious pathos, as though a tender-hearted woman were speaking. Among all his works of fiction 'Esmond' is my special favourite. In that delightful romance would seem to be united every quality of excellence of which literary art applied to such a purpose is capable. From first to last the reader's interest is sustained. The very scenery and material incidents of the story are described with a dexterous limner's skill. Supreme irony, radiant wit, a keen sense of the picturesque, and a thorough knowledge of the world are blended in these pages—tempered and purified, moreover, by a deep religious feeling which pervades the whole—like the distant strains of a cathedral organ heard through the hum and turmoil of city life.

. . . .

I said at the beginning of this chapter that I was a desultory reader, and the very books which I have selected for mention will show the hap-hazard nature of my studies. Studies indeed! How can a man be called a student who only reads to amuse himself? Books are often described as companions, but they have this advantage over their human rivals, that you can choose them according to your mood. One must be in a serious vein to appreciate Bacon's 'Essays' or enjoy Milton's poetry (I once read 'Paradise Lost' right through, but to say the truth I don't often find myself up to that level). At another time one is content with Byron and Hain Friswell.

There have been days in my life when Lord Chesterfield's Letters entertained me, and though your up-to-date 'masher' would be bored by their perusal, let me add that there is a good deal of advice given by that astute nobleman from which our modern British youth might still derive some profit.

By way of a fireside diversion at Christmas, I once took down a volume of the Arabian Nights (Lane's edition), and lighting upon the ingenious story of Prince Kamar-Ez-Zemán and the Princess Budoor, which I had forgotten, was proceeding to read it aloud, when the nature of some of the incidents described, and the presence of my Aunt Diana (a spinster lady from Clapham), compelled me to assume a violent fit of coughing under plea of which I was enabled to stop, but only just in time.

The quaint colloquies in dear old Isaac Walton's 'Compleat Angler,' Carlyle's rugged eloquence—the rattling humour of Sheridan, Lamb's thoughtful essays, Longfellow's musical verse, Ruskin's delightful paradox, Nathaniel Hawthorne's charming prose, and Mark Twain's laugh-provoking fun, not to mention a score of other literary treasures, are all within reach on my bookshelves. Scarcely a night passes but I take some volume down, and presently a fragrant incense arises in its honour. It is from my pipe.

CHAPTER VI

MY SANCTUM

My sanctum is devoted to a great many purposes which vary with the time of the day. My own occupation of it is chiefly limited to the early morning and late evening hours. Sometimes a letter arriving by the first post requires an immediate answer; sometimes a cheque has to be drawn, sometimes household matters need attention, or domestics want a lecture.

It is here that I interview Susan, who has broken five wine-glasses, chipped several pieces off the best dinner service, cracked three gas globes, and snapped a couple of window-sash lines—all since last quarter day. Susan is a tall and superior looking servant, with a Diana-like presence and a charming manner. I remonstrate with her—not for the first time. I point out the error of her ways. I remind her that some day she may have a house of her own, and I ask her how she would like to have her own property knocked about and destroyed after this fashion. She admits that it would be extremely unsatisfactory. I give her an approximate idea of what these breakages cost me in the course of a year, and I appeal to her better feelings. On this she generally weeps, expresses the utmost contrition and an earnest resolve to be more careful for the future—a promise which, to do her justice, she strictly keeps for at least a fortnight afterwards.

Into this room, too, are ushered from time to time mysterious visitors who, considerately choosing the breakfast or dinner hour for their calls, desire to see me on private business, the nature of which they decline to state at the front door, and only on pressure reveal their names. Sometimes it is the enterprising emissary of a patentee, who produces a new gas burner warranted to emit a flame yielding twice the ordinary amount of light at half the usual price, or recommends an ingenious apparatus combining all the essentials of a window-cleaner, fire-escape, and douche-bath at the modest price of 6*l.* 10*s.*

Sometimes it is a pale and interesting youth who, owing to the sudden death of both parents and the inhuman conduct of an uncle, has walked all the way from Macclesfield to London in the hope of obtaining employment as a type-writer or amanuensis. With this end in view he suggests that I should furnish him with the names and addresses of a few personal friends to whom he might present himself with a line of introduction from me. On my declining to accede to this request, he thinks I might at least oblige him with a pair of boots, and finding that I am not disposed to do so, he abruptly retires and walks off with one of my umbrellas instead.

Then there is the venerable marine engineer who served on board H.M.S. 'Bellerophon' (which he pronounces regardless of quantities) and alluding to a gallant admiral of my acquaintance as an 'old shipmate' of his, produces a greasy little account book in which are entered various names and subscriptions ranging from a half-crown to one guinea. To this list he would like to add my autograph if only for the amount of five shillings, but as he turns over the leaves, I notice that his hand shakes a good deal and that since he began to speak the room is filled with an unwonted odour of Jamaica rum. In these circumstances I think it prudent to defer my donation until next week in order that I may meanwhile make inquiries into the case. He reluctantly assents, promising to return in a few days, but, strange to say, I never see him again.

It is in my 'sanctum' that I interview my builders: I use the plural number, not because I employ more than one at a time, but because I have had so many—about seven, I think—since I first became a tenant of this house, which costs me about *50l.* a year in repairs. They have varied much in personal appearance, and demeanour, in the scale of their charges and the nature of their advice ; but if they have one attribute in common, I should say it was incapacity.

It must not be supposed that I am one of those householders who want everything done ' on the cheap, as the phrase goes. On the contrary, I am always prepared to give a good price for good work. But unfortunately I don't always find that one secures the other. I have tried builders in a large way of business (one of them used to drive up to my door in his carriage) as well as in a small way. I have tried solemn reflective builders, who look as if they were mentally working out a problem in hydraulics when one wants a new tap fixed over the scullery sink ; dapper cheerful builders, who talk as if they could remodel the drains and fix a new kitchen range by the day after to-morrow ; scientific builders, who have wonderful theories about ventilation which result in five cross draughts on each floor ; expeditious builders, who go to work with such promptitude that the front door begins to blister exactly twenty-four hours after it has been fresh painted ; careful and steady-going builders, whose men take a fortnight to paper a bedroom ; and artistic builders, who conceive that mauve and pea-green afford a pleasing contrast in the decoration of a boudoir.

But perhaps the most dangerous type of his class

is your thoroughly practical man. An ingenious artificer of this kind once superintended the hanging of a heavy set of bookshelves on a wall just over the easy-chair in my study. When they were well filled with books and surmounted by a life-size plaster bust of Minerva, he congratulated me on the result. He said it was a capital job. It very nearly became a capital offence. A few months afterwards, as I was sitting over the fire, when luckily my pipe went out, I rose to re-light it, when I was startled by an awful crash. The shelves with their contents had fallen down *en masse* and my chair was covered with fragments of Pallas Athene's head!

I was once recommended to employ a Co-operative Society of Builders and Decorators on the ground that members of this guild work directly for their customers without the intervention of a 'middle-man,' who, it was urged, frequently appropriated a large proportion of the profits. Relieved from this oppression, the co-operatives were able to do work entrusted to them at a much more reasonable rate than would be charged by a master-builder. This appeared so obvious that when my bath-room wanted repair I put the job into the hands of the guild, and I found their workmen very co-operative indeed.

One undertook to re-enamel the bath, which is a very heavy one, and as it was conveyed downstairs, left indications of its progress to the front door in the form of streaks and scratches on the staircase wall. The natural result of this was that a painter and paper-hanger from the same establishment were sent (at my cost) to repair the damage. When the bath was replaced a carpenter came to re-fix the wood fittings. In the execution of this duty he ingeniously managed to step inside the bath with hob-nailed boots, which laid the foundation for a future job in the plumber's interest.

Then the French polisher arrived and spent a day or two over the mahogany which, to do him justice, he left in beautiful condition, though he splashed the window with some of his varnish. That, however, as he pointed out, was almost inevitable, and could soon be put right by the window-cleaner—a very active man, who was so energetic over his work that he broke one of the window panes. To make amends for this accident he recommended a co-operative glazier. The glazier came, but found that he could not quite complete his job without re-summoning the carpenter, who, with a true co-operative instinct, rested his hot gluepot on the surface of the polished mahogany.

These casualties, considered in relation to the total sum which I had eventually to pay for the repair of my bath-room, led me to conclude that the co-operative system, though admirably calculated to provide employment for the masses, was not quite so economical in its result as I had anticipated.

I have said that I use my sanctum for correspondence, which certainly ought not in my case to be voluminous. Yet somehow I get through a vast amount of stationery, and as for my store of postage stamps it is always being replenished. There was an idle saying in the days of my youth, that most letters answer themselves if you only leave them alone. But I can never do so. The bare fact of a note being addressed to me on any matter—however unimportant—suggests a reply. This is probably the result of a pampered conscience, but I send it nevertheless.

I have a worse weakness—which is that of keeping letters. My writing-table contains nearly a dozen drawers alphabetically labelled. This enables me to classify my papers, so that I can find any one of them at a minute's notice. All this is very methodical, but the result is appalling. My drawers are crammed with letters which I have not the courage to destroy. Some are souvenirs of the absent; others are mementos of the dead; some recall cheery days of friendship with those who, alas! are no longer friends; others relate to circumstances of which one wishes to preserve a record. Some inscribed in round childish characters are associated with recollections of the past. Others are penned by hands which one feels instinctively will soon write no more. I weed these papers from time to time—consign a few to the fire—but I can't burn them all. *Litera scripta manet.*

As for pamphlets, newspaper cuttings, trade circulars, recipes, catalogues, manuals, and odd numbers of magazines which for some special reason I wish to keep for reference, their number is legion, but by the aid of pigeon-holes, scrap-books, and folios, I manage to put them in order. Tidiness is perhaps a cheap virtue, but you can't manage a household without it. I don't believe people who say that they have no time to be neat. Your sloven wastes half his time in fruitless searching.

I can't answer for other rooms in Terra-cottage, but except when Susan in her weekly dusting thrusts my unpaid bills into the *jardinière*, puts the advertising coal merchant's circular into the card rack, and replaces my Balzac (upside down) between two volumes of Colenso's 'Pentateuch' in the bookcase, I flatter myself that the contents of my sanctum are methodically arranged.

Account keeping is another minor virtue often held in great contempt by superior people. If I had been a genius, or possessed more money than I knew what to do with, I daresay that I should never have cultivated this useful art. But as my income is a modest one—though it reaches the conventional standard of competence represented by four figures, I derive some amusement from the practice. It does not occupy me more than ten minutes in a day, and has gradually educated me into a domestic financier.

Once a quarter I resolve myself into a committee for supply. I prepare my own budget, based on trustworthy statistics. I estimate surpluses; provide for deficits; propose a reduction on certain votes until an explanation is afforded, and then carry my own resolutions *nem. con.* At Christmas I compare receipts and expenditure in former years with those of the past twelve months, and become first lord of the treasury, chancellor of the exchequer, and auditor-general all rolled into one. Sometimes my budget enables me to carry a little balance forward—and then I congratulate myself on my successful administration.

During my occasional absence this favourite retreat of mine is invaded by my wife, who reads the 'Times' there, and by my Cousin Bridget, who, though she has a room of her own, finds a convenient repository on my shelves for her grammar books and dictionaries. Cousin Bridget is about thirty-two years of age—more or less. If you should say less I shall not contradict you, and I am sure that she won't. She is an orphan, blessed with ample means, and accomplished. She can talk French and Italian. She has also learnt Norse, and conducts an imaginary correspondence with some one in the Loffoden Islands. I can't think what she writes about, but I have a shrewd suspicion that the Aurora Borealis and the Viking dynasty form the principal topics for discussion in her letters.

She is supposed to entertain hopes of bringing the force of moral and intellectual culture to bear upon the Laps, and has spent some weeks among that interesting people, studying their domestic habits and means of subsistence, which seem to be characterised —so far as I can learn—by a supreme disregard for the conventionalities of life rather than by any individual charm.

Cousin Bridget can paint, too, with great dexterity in water colours, and might have made a livelihood in that way if her ancestors had followed the fine arts professionally. But, being wise in their generation, they adopted quite a different mode of making money, with the result that Cousin Bridget inherits a handsome competence, and is happily not under the necessity of parting with her sketches. She has also considerable taste for music, and there is a tradition that she used once to play and sing, but of late years a kindly fate has caused her to abandon pianoforte practice, which as a daily custom in a small house would have been— well, not exactly an unmixed joy.

Cousin Bridget is very fond of travelling. She

goes abroad once or twice a year, and has a peculiar talent for planning out routes months before her departure. Next to irregular Italian verbs, I think that the pages of Bradshaw afford her the most attractive object for study. She understands that erudite periodical thoroughly; knows the advantage which this or that line of route presents in comparison with another; what railway company affords the greatest facilities to the travelling public; where first-class carriages are indispensable; where you may make shift with second; how many buffet restaurants there are between Calais and Bâle; which is the best hotel at Bucharest; and how long it will take you to reach Niagara.

She delights in solving intricate itinerary problems, such as to ascertain at what station it would be most convenient to meet a friend who leaves Glasgow for London by the night mail and wishes to spend an hour or so at Carlisle, when Bridget is on the way to Scarborough. She makes nice calculations which enable her to start from Boulogne in time to see the Coliseum at Rome by moonlight, or arrive in Venice on the eve of an annual water *fête*. She knows the names of all the steamers which run on the Norwegian coast, and at what points they leave the land-locked sea to venture into open water. She could tell you at a moment's notice what o'clock it is at Moscow when it is a quarter past noon at Tours.

Cousin Bridget's travelling apparatus is elaborate and complex. It includes two kinds of hats and a sleeping cap; a railway rug, a foot-warmer and an air cushion; a basket of fruit, a bottle of arnica, three umbrellas and a sketching stool, which no one but herself could ever fold up. She has incontrovertible views as to which is the best seat in a railway carriage, assuming that the train is proceeding in a given direction, and provided that the width of the gauge, the state of the weather, and the hour of the day have all been carefully considered. But even these calculations are occasionally upset by the presence of a travelling baby, to which she has a deep-rooted aversion, and which will account for her generally avoiding the 'Ladies' compartment.'

Cousin Bridget is never idle, and for many years past she has devoted herself to the study of various subjects, each of which forms for the time being the all-absorbing hobby of her life. Female suffrage, the tidal theory, hypnotism, fern culture, and the doctrines of Confucius, not to mention stenography and primogeniture, have successively occupied her attention. She has a theory respecting the Man in the Iron Mask, and at one time thought of writing an essay on the grape-cure, from which she was only dissuaded by an eminent theosophist, who considered that treatment fraught with danger to the patient's future condition in a higher plane.

But among Cousin Bridget's many virtues punctuality and tidiness cannot be reckoned. If 'Order is Heaven's first law,' I fear she has little chance at present of becoming an angel. With all her extraordinary aptitude for planning trips and interpreting time-tables, a more unmethodical young lady I never knew. Her books, letters, manuscripts, shop bills and parcels are distributed with an impartial hand in every room alike. Her boots, gloves, and hand-bag turn up promiscuously in unexpected places.

Our breakfast hour being (nominally) nine o'clock, Cousin Bridget generally comes down at a quarter to ten. She appears late at lunch on the plea that she has been mending her veil. When the bell rings as a signal to dress for dinner she is suddenly reminded that she ought to have written to a friend in Aberdeen last month, and forthwith proceeds to compose a letter. She is always mislaying her bracelets. As for her watch, it has been to my certain knowledge hopelessly lost seven times between Christmas and Lady Day, but miraculously rediscovered after a day's search in out-of-the-way places, such as a bonnet box, a sandwich case, behind a sofa cushion, or in the hollow of a muff. It is like a conjuring trick.

She once left a cheque for ten guineas for three weeks in a volume of 'Macaulay's Essays,' and actually wrote to the Post Office authorities requesting them to trace the letter in which she believed she had remitted it.

Cousin Bridget seems to entertain a belief that her correspondents' private notes were intended for book-markers; that the mantelpiece spill jar is an excellent receptacle for paid bills; that letters can be most conveniently written on the cushion of a drawing-room sofa, or, if the writer should prefer a standing position, on the top shelf of the dinner-waggon, especially if she has her back to the light.

She apparently considers that table drawers look more picturesque when left half open, and that cupboard doors in order to ensure ventilation should never be shut.

Possessed of an ample wardrobe, Cousin Bridget is never able to regulate her attire by the nice fluctuations of the thermometer. Thus, after starting out for a walk, she finds the air too chilly for her summer jacket, and is filled with regret that she had not put on her mantle. She hurries back to make the change, but half an hour afterwards she complains that the mantle is too warm, and that she must carry it on her arm.

Cousin Bridget is very choice in lavender-water

and eau-de-Cologne. Her stock of homœopathic medicines, too, is prodigious. There is scarcely a human ailment for which she does not possess a specific. There are globules for catarrh and neuralgia; globules for dyspepsia and headache; globules for insomnia and laryngitis. I have never actually seen any labelled for chilblains, but I should not be surprised if they exist.

My own personal experience does not enable me to bear testimony to the effect of these several remedies, but, judging from the experiments made on our servants, I should say that it was at least harmless. Out of twenty-five cases treated last year, one certainly resulted in a cure, but whether it was brought about by a globule or (as I am rather inclined to believe) by the patient being kept in bed all day, with a liberal supply of linseed-meal poultices, I am unable to state.

My cousin has strong political views, but they are liable to fluctuations. During a Conservative administration her sentiments incline to Liberalism, and she has even been known to speak in favour of Home Rule. But as soon as the Gladstonians come into office no one of her sex could advocate Tory doctrines with greater warmth. If ever women should be admitted into Parliament, and she enters the House of Commons as a lady member, she will most assuredly be found on the

Opposition Bench. This tendency to social polemics is the keynote of her character.

Although naturally of the most amiable disposition, she finds an inexhaustible pleasure in argument. This peculiarity runs through everything—no matter what the subject under discussion may be—the administration of charity, the state of the weather, apostolical succession or bi-metallism, the total abstinence question or the merits of the last novel: it is sufficient for you to express your views and Cousin Bridget, from mere force of habit, will at once deliver herself of a contrary opinion. If you concede a point it is one to which, as she tells you, she does not attach much importance. It is the major issue which she insists on. But if you agree with her altogether her enthusiasm somewhat wanes, and I think she is disappointed. Nature intended her for a special pleader. She is not given to squabbling, but she dearly loves to contend. Between ourselves I call her the 'junior wrangler,' and I believe she is rather proud of the title.

But if Bridget is a Philistine among her fellow creatures, she is a slave to her four-footed pets. The amount of time and attention which she devotes to our little dog 'Pixie' surpasses belief. He is an affectionate little rascal all round, but he regards Bridget as his especial champion and playmate. She takes him daily for a walk, clad during the winter in a coat of her own making. She propitiates him with choice fragments of bread and butter, sly lumps of sugar and surreptitious saucers of milk. He lies outside her bedroom door in the morning, and takes his carriage exercise in her company.

So, taking these redeeming qualities into consideration, I have made my cousin free of the 'sanctum' on the express understanding that it shall be kept tidy while she uses it, and under a penalty which would involve the disallowance of apricot jam—a confection much to her taste for breakfast. Other ladies rarely enter the room, but it is a favourite haunt of any bachelor friends who have been dining with us, and who join me there over a pipe in the evening hours. Even Bob Goldie, who lives in a Belgravian palace with a billiard and smoking divan twice as big as my drawing-room, and who, I have no doubt, regards me in the light of a respectable pauper—even this affluent youth, I say, as he flings himself into my easy chair and lights a cigarette, looks round him with an air of approval, and observes that it is 'a doosid comfortable little den, don't ye know; a jolly little corner for a smoke, with books and papers and soda-water handy, and after all what more can a fellow want?'

Then Goldie proceeds to entertain me with an account of his recent pastimes and acquisitions—what a jolly time he spent at Henley in the house-boat built for him by Messrs. Rowlock and Stretcher; how he managed to secure a capital pair of greys for his landau last week at Tattersalls': 'three hundred and fifty was the figure, old chap, and very cheap at the price, mind you!' He informs me with great gravity that he has taken a Scotch moor for the autumn, and promises to put me up if I like to run down for a few days' shooting (I, who have not handled a gun for the last twenty years!). He describes the additions which he has made to his country house in Gloucestershire, and mentions with a certain pride, pardonable at his age, that he has just been elected a member of the Malachite Club, which, as we all know, is a mark of great social distinction. And yet this young Crœsus is simple and unaffected, puts on no 'side' in my sanctum, but puffs away at his cigarettes and praises my Glenlivet whiskey as if he had nothing so good in his own cellar.

On another evening, perhaps, I find myself hob-nobbing with my old friend Stippler, who entered the schools of the Royal Academy with me—we won't say how many years ago. I fear that Stippler has not met with much success in the practice of his art. It is not for want of industry. He has worked hard all his life and years ago made a decent income by his brush, but public taste has changed and he has not kept up with the times. There is no demand now for *genre* pictures—scenes from rustic life and such like simple subjects, to which he devotes himself. He sent three canvases to the Royal Academy this year and not one was hung.

'To make a hit nowadays, old man,' says he rather sadly, 'one must be either a tip-top genius or a sensationalist in painting, and I am neither. I know my work is old-fashioned—perhaps commonplace. There are hundreds of young fellows now who paint as well as I—some of them a great deal better—and they can't sell their things. How can I expect to do so? The fact is there are too many of us by half. I always hated art cliques, and I am not "in" with the Press. It is lucky that I made a little money years ago, or I should be in a bad way now.

And then we fall to talking of old times, when his 'Pyramus and Thisbe' won the Royal Academy Gold Medal and was hung on the line; of the winter we passed together in Rome, and how we enjoyed the Carnival there a quarter of a century ago.

Eheu fugaces labuntur anni! Stippler's hair is not so bushy as it was once, and his beard is streaked here and there with silvery lines. Perhaps, as he says, there are too many painters nowadays. Or, may be, the public taste for modern pictorial art is not so easily satisfied as formerly. Your collectors will have nothing but first-rate work. And then, alack! comes the question, what *is* first-rate? To many a *soi-disant* connoisseur I fancy it means something that he has never seen before—something which, either in choice of subject, or method of handling, or scheme of colour, or extravagance of form, has startled him by its piquancy—just as a new sauce might please the jaded appetite of an epicure, or the latest novelty from Paris commend itself to a mere woman of fashion at her milliner's. Old canons of style and grace are forgotten—old standards of excellence are set aside.

The one essential condition of success for a *fin-de-siècle* picture is that it shall be original. Group your figures in constrained attitudes—enshroud them with fog or deck them in all the colours of the rainbow: paint your skies red and your meadows blue: show us a sea without ships, knights without courage, youth without joy, love-making without beauty, drapery without texture—'impressions' good, bad, or indifferent—no matter so long as they are ORIGINAL!

Sometimes my spare chair is occupied by my quondam schoolfellow, Tom Vicary. Tom was pitchforked into public life at an early age and, not being a particularly ambitious man, wisely deemed a modest but certain stipend preferable to that income of 'unknown quantity' which he might have earned by a professional career.

Tom is in the service of a well-known European

Company and has gradually risen to a good position in his department. His occupation interests him and he would be as happy as the days are long, but there is one drawback to his comfort. He has an unsatisfactory colleague. According to Tom's account the man is vain, selfish, and suspicious.

Tom does almost all the English work of the office, but whatever credit accrues from it goes to the foreign secretary, De Sansjoie, whose 'zealous services' are kept before the shareholders, while Vicary's name is never mentioned.

'I wouldn't mind that so much,' says Tom, good-naturedly, 'if he were barely civil in our daily intercourse. But in ten years of official life, this egotistical alien has rarely opened his lips to me save on matters of business, or answered a question with common courtesy. How can you deal with such a man?' cries Tom, his face flushing with honest indignation. 'Sometimes, after a hard day's work in the City I lie awake at night thinking of his ridiculous conceit, his contemptible jealousy and hateful rudeness. It almost makes one——'

When Tom reaches this stage of righteous anger I venture to replenish his tumbler, and give him a fresh pipe of my choice smoking mixture, which he greatly appreciates, and which has a marvellous effect in soothing his nerves. Ah, good, fragrant, comforting tobacco! What would some of us poor harassed mortals do without it? I vow that there have been moments in my life when my pipe has seemed to me the truest friend, the most genial companion, the kindest consoler that I ever had. It helps one to enjoy a book, to appreciate scenery, to allay fatigue and promote digestion. It shares one's joys and tempers one's grief.

And yet there are wiseacres who have described tobacco as unwholesome and even demoralising! No one but a fool smokes to excess. You might as well be a glutton at dinner, or go to bed every night fuddled. The perpetual whiffing of cigarettes is, no doubt, a bad practice. Ladies naturally object to it, and I have no patience with men who indulge in this selfish habit between the acts at a theatre—when they ought to be talking to their fair companions. Even at garden parties and in places of public resort it is open to objection. But after dinner, in the quiet hours of the evening, by a cheerful fire in your 'study,' when the children are gone to 'bye-bye' and your good wife is absorbed in a novel upstairs, who could object to an honest pipe or two, taken as a gentle soporific, and just reward to the bread-winner, after a hard day's work?

Occasionally my good doctor drops in—unprofessionally—for a chat on his way homewards of an evening after seeing his last patient. Joliffe is much too sensible a man to object to smoking or any other harmless physical indulgence in moderation. When I was recovering under his judicious care from a severe attack of influenza last winter, he was positively delighted to find me with a cigar in my mouth. 'That's a good sign,' exclaimed the cheery practitioner as he entered my 'sanctum.' 'There is an odour of convalescence about this room. Whenever I find my patients relishing a quiet whiff I know they are getting better.

Joliffe is no believer in total abstinence. I have known him prescribe a pint of dry champagne without a qualm. He even recognises in certain cases the medicinal properties of old Burgundy. He does not dose you with unnecessary physic. Indeed, we came to an understanding on this point years ago. I took him into my confidence. I told him that I knew quite well how many invalids—old ladies especially—think that a medical man has never earned his fee unless he leaves a prescription behind him—but that, for my own part, I believed more in his advice than in concoctions made up by the chemist. A tonic or anodyne if you please—a harmless pill now and then to keep the liver in order—a hint as to diet and habits of life—a cheerful assurance that your symptoms are not so grave as you suppose them to be, and that you will be right again in a few days—that is the sort of treatment for nervous and hypochondriacal subjects, of whom I confess myself to be one.

'My dear fellow,' said Joliffe, laughing, 'I only wish that more of my patients would take the same line. It would save me a deal of trouble.'

The sight of that man's face is enough to re-assure any *malade imaginaire.* A few minutes' talk with him—and, for all his large practice, he never seems in a hurry—inspires one with fresh confidence. I feel all the better for his company. That is the kind of physician I like—none of your long-faced gloomy advisers. It is the old story of *Dr. Tant-mieux* and *Dr. Tant-pis* which I read as a child, in La Fontaine's 'Fables,' ever so long ago! And if I should have a serious illness, it is Dr. Tant-mieux whom I would wish to see at my bedside.

Sometimes I find myself alone—yes, quite alone—in my study, and though I am naturally of the gregarious kind, and like to see my fellow creatures about me, there are moments in every man's life when he wants to be left to himself. For instance, there is the musing hour, just before bed time, when one is tired of conversation, tired of reading, and the last whiff of smoke ascends from an extinguished pipe. I knock the ashes out and fall to thinking of old times.

. . . . . .

Of childhood perhaps, and the dear, good, unselfish soul to whom I owe my life and all that makes life worth living. One portrait of her still in blooming youth, smiles down on me from the opposite wall, and close to my arm chair hangs another, sketched by myself, towards the end of her well-spent life. *Alma, pia Mater!*

Of boyhood, and the rough but jolly schooldays at Eastminster, with bright-eyed cheery companions, some of whom have long since passed away, while others are growing grey and sober.

Of youth, with all its pleasures, follies, dangers, long-repented faults, and bitter lessons of experience.

Of early manhood, with its vain ambition, trials, and struggles—hopes that have vanished, friends who have proved unfriendly, schemes which have collapsed, work which was fruitless.

Of wiser middle-age, with its better knowledge of the world, its calmer philosophy, its more tempered joys, its late but all-sufficient success, its more accurate measure of humanity, its keener sense of duty, its blessed feeling of content.

And then I light my candle and go upstairs gratefully to bed.

CHAPTER VII

GOING TO ROOST

Country cousins are always welcome at Terra-cottage, but, as ours are for the most part unmarried and our house is not a large one, we are selfish enough to keep the biggest bedroom for our own use. It is a cheerful and airy apartment on the second floor, with two windows overlooking the Square garden. In summer time, when the trees are in full leaf and the birds are chirping outside, the prospect, surveyed at dawn with a clear sky overhead, is almost rural.

The walls of the room are papered with my favourite 'solanum' pattern and hung with prints, photographs, and family portraits. My wife insisted on having what cabinet-makers call an 'over-mantel' for the fireplace, panelled with little mirrors of bevelled glass and provided with shelves on which a choice selection of Bretby ware and other knicknacks are displayed by her with great ingenuity.

The central feature is a clock considerably advanced in years, but possessed of a wonderful constitution. We bought it when we first went into housekeeping, and in the days of its youth it used to stand on the chimney-piece of my study. Whether the smoke there disagreed with its interior or what I don't know, but it fell into bad habits. Sometimes it lost half an hour a day, and the next week, by way of atoning for this waste of time, it would progress with such alarming rapidity that a young and inexperienced parlourmaid once prepared the table for lunch soon after breakfast. Then the minute hand had a difference with the hour hand, which declined to be hurried in this fashion and remained sulking at 6 P.M. for a fortnight while its more energetic companion went on its way rejoicing and alone. Occasionally the clock so far forgot its dignity as to strike incontinently at odd and unexpected times, pretended to be an electric bell, and went on ringing with such violence that I had to put it into a cupboard until it had run down.

Curiously enough, when it was exiled to our bedroom in order to make room for a smarter and more trustworthy timepiece, the old clock, repenting of its evil ways, became a reformed character, and, in spite of its age, kept excellent time. It is still subject to slight ebullitions of temper, which occasionally have the effect of making it tick more loudly than usual, but, on the whole, I regard it now as a steady and well-conducted clock.

One of the most conspicuous features in our bedroom is my wife's toilet-table, with a swing-glass in the middle, which has a habit of presenting itself unexpectedly at an angle of forty-five degrees in the wrong direction, and a little set of drawers which baffle human ingenuity to open when you are in a hurry, and which, having been once opened, require on an average about five minutes apiece to shut. They contain innumerable articles, ranging from gelatine lozenges to patent hair pins, classified on a system which would be perfect but for the fact that our maid Phœbe, an ingenious creature who loves variety, delights in shifting their contents whenever the drawers are dusted. I believe that she derives a certain satisfaction from foreseeing that her master, when searching for seidlitz powders, will find them changed into lip-salve and court plaster. It is like a bit of professional magic. Maskelyne and Cook could hardly beat it.

According to my old fashioned notions, a dressing-table should be covered with a plain white cloth for the reception of a few toilet articles, leaving space to put down a letter, a tumbler, a bunch of keys, or any extra thing which comes to hand. But my wife's dressing-table is so crowded with knicknacks that you can scarcely move one without knocking down the others. To be sure, they are all very elegant. In the centre there is a silver tray (at least, it is supposed to be silver, but I rather suspect electro-plate). This is destined to receive two large hair brushes, with highly-embossed silver backs. They are so precious that when not in use they are covered over with a satin napkin trimmed with white lace. Then there is a silver pomade-jar, a silver powder-box (never wanted, I am thankful to say), a silver scent-case, a silver pincushion, a silver hand-glass and a silver toast-rack, apparently intended to hold letters.

As if this were not enough, there are at each end of the table two silver photograph-stands of singular design and workmanship. Each is provided with folding doors of lattice-work, which, when closed, have the effect of a miniature cage. My portrait is in one and that of my mother-in-law in the other. Now, I don't so much mind seeing my mother-in-law in a cage. Indeed, there is a sense of security about it which is almost pleasant. But I don't like to see my own features peeping out through a grille. It looks as if one had been incarcerated for felony. But there —it is no use arguing with woman. My wife—Heaven bless her!—is very proud of her toys, and it is my belief that she won't be content until she possesses a silver sponge-bath.

I have travelled north, south, east, and west in Europe, and have slept at many far-famed hostelries on the Continent, but I have never yet found anything equal in comfort to a modern English bed. There is always some drawback to a foreign bedstead. It is either too high or too low, or too broad or too short. You graze your shins in getting into it, or pull the coverlet after you in getting out. The pillows are either as hard as a football or else they have a handful of feathers at each end and nothing whatever in the middle. The eider-down slides off in the night, and your feet come into contact with a cold footboard in the morning. The sheets refuse to be tucked in and wrinkle into corrugations under your body or exhale a mingled perfume of stale starch and damp straw. It may be insular prejudice, but with all the charm and novelty of foreign scenes by daylight, I prefer my nights at home.

Of all the ills that flesh is heir to, insomnia seems to me among the worst. I think I must have suffered occasionally from it as a child, for I remember my nurse telling me that the best way to induce sleep was to imagine oneself alone, on the top of a high mountain, looking down upon grazing sheep. I believed so firmly in this soporific that it generally had the desired effect.

Thank goodness, I have no need now to climb imaginary hills or watch the movements of a phantom flock. In twenty minutes, or, at most, half an hour, after I 'turn in,' as the sailors say, Morpheus leads me gently into dreamland. What a wonderful country it is! how strangely inhabited; how full of marvels which do not surprise; of joys which do not unduly elate; of griefs which seem tolerable; of easy morals, which seldom shock; of grotesque incidents which one accepts as natural; of inconsistencies which are never puzzling.

You are of no particular age in dreamland; you meet friends, long since dead, whom you knew in childhood, and talk to them familiarly. It never occurs to you to ask them why they have revisited this sphere, nor what has become of them for all these years. If, in order to render their reappearance probable, you become yourself again rejuvenated, your later life passes out of your memory. But, in any case, they do not seem a bit older than they were twenty or thirty years ago. You may have followed them to the grave, but in dreamland that doesn't signify. You have been under a wrong impression. It is all right, and they are alive again. That's all you know or care about. It is very pleasant to meet again, and you don't stop to ask troublesome questions.

Although I have had many quarrels and more than one serious encounter in my sleep, it has never been with the departed. They are always agreeable, and generally glad to see me. The ethics of dreamland are very peculiar. I don't remember having stolen anything there, but I have often committed bigamy without the slightest remorse. I was once wrongfully accused of homicide—I don't remember on what grounds, nor who had been assassinated. I believe the evidence was entirely circumstantial, but I have no recollection of a trial. I only know that I was sentenced to be hung, and that my friends had interceded in vain for me; my execution was to take place on the following day—but luckily I awoke before it was carried into effect.

On another occasion I was taken prisoner during the Franco-German war, together with several other Englishmen. What we had been doing on the field of battle I can't imagine, but, for my own part, I feel pretty sure that I had not been fighting. However, we were all pinioned and brought before Moltke, who, in the most arbitrary and offhand manner, condemned us to be decapitated. The executioner had a horribly long sword of mediæval appearance—such a weapon as might have been wielded in the crusades. He used this with great dexterity on several of his victims, and then had ten minutes' interval allowed him for refreshment.

When he had finished his lunch, Moltke, who was evidently in a hurry, called out: 'Now, my lads, sharp's the word. Who is next on the list?'

'Mr. Asterisk Blank,' said the executioner cheerfully, mentioning a well-known member of our British Parliament. 'Now, Mr. Blank, kneel down, if you please,' said Moltke, lighting a cigarette; and when I say "Three," you know,' he added to the executioner, 'you can let fly!'

I noticed that he spoke English remarkably well.

Mr. Blank knelt down. 'ONE—TWO—THREE!' cried Moltke. Ah! the sword descended on the hapless victim, but, instead of taking the member's head off, it only sliced off the top like a Dutch cheese. To our great surprise, Mr. Blank did not groan or fall, but remained in a kneeling position, and, looking up at the executioner, said, rather testily, 'Now then, stoopid!' 'Beg pardon, sir!' exclaimed the executioner, 'my hands are getting rather tired. I'll have another try.

'ONE—TWO—THREE!!' again shouted Moltke. Once more the sword descended, but it only took off another slice of the kneeling man's head; and this time he spoke more angrily. 'Come, I say,' cried he, 'this really won't do; I'm not going to stay here all day while you are bungling in this manner. Finish me off at once, and be done with it.' And he did so.

'Next man,' cried Moltke, rubbing his hands.

'Mr. Jack Easel,' said the executioner.

It was an awful moment, but I determined to

make a last effort to save myself. I flung myself at Moltke's feet. 'Spare me, General,' I said; 'I am young and intelligent. Who knows?—I may be of service to you in the war.' 'Oh, that's all damned nonsense!' answered Moltke, peevishly. 'Executioner, do your duty.' ONE—TWO . . . THREE! It struck—I don't mean the sword, but the timepiece. It struck three o'clock A.M., and I awoke, trembling.

There are two curious and inexplicable dreams by which I am haunted at certain intervals. One is that I am on the Continent, where I have been staying for many months—indeed, the best part of a year—but that, instead of occupying myself with sketching, making literary notes, &c. &c., I have been sadly wasting my time. I am in some interesting old foreign town, where there are endless objects of interest. I am obliged to start for England by an early train the next morning, and during the interval I have to visit five important churches, examine the contents of three picture galleries, ascend the cathedral tower, take a walk on the boulevards, inspect the local museum, buy presents for all my relations, pay my hotel bill, pack my luggage, and write up my diary—all in one afternoon. I am naturally appalled at the prospect, and generally end by doing nothing. I hire a cicerone the next day to show me the nearest way to the railway station. It takes him several hours to find it, and I always arrive too late for my train.

The other dream is that I am at Eastminster School again: that I have overstayed my time there, and am about one or two and twenty years of age; that I have to pass an examination to qualify myself for a studentship at one of the Universities; and that I am hopelessly backward. I have forgotten the little Greek which I once knew: I am puzzled over a chorus in Hecuba. I cannot translate a page of the Iliad to save my life. I have lost the secret of extracting cube roots and can no more manage a quadratic equation than I could fly. I feel certain of being 'ploughed,' I have already broken down in a vivâ voce and left half my paper questions unanswered. Time is nearly up and I have just ten minutes left wherein to describe concisely the nature of the Binomial Theorem and write an essay on the Greek particles. The conviction that I shall be beaten by boys three or four years younger than myself fills me with a sense of shame and degradation. I rush in despair from the school with the notion of jumping into the river. But I generally awake before doing so.

Those two dreams, with certain variations of detail, fall to my lot from time to time, and they are certainly unpleasant. But, generally speaking, the visions of my sleep are serene and pleasant ones.

Among the exploded follies of proverbial philosophy surely the monstrous rule which prescribes to mortals a fixed and uniform period for rest is unsurpassed in absurdity. The old saying used to be 'Six hours for a man, seven for a woman, and eight for a fool.' Vastly well, my ancient sage, but first tell me to what sort of man and what sort of woman you presume to dictate this advice? Have age, health, temperament, climate, season, circumstances, local conditions, and habits of life nothing to do with the question? Why, you might as well weigh out the daily food of Daniel Lambert and the living skeleton, and tell each to eat that exact amount, neither more nor less. Some of us require, and ought to have, fifty per cent more of sleep than others.

What you call laziness may be the natural result of nervous exhaustion. Legitimate energy means perfect health. Indolence may be a wise and recuperative provision of nature. Morbid activity may lead to Earlswood or consign you to mother earth prematurely. 'Early to bed and early to rise.' By all means, my worthy mentor, if you can manage it. But think of the 'Times' office at 2 A.M., when, according to your theory sub-editors, leader-writers, telegraphists, compositors, printers, and newsmen ought all to be snoring. And yet you expect your morning paper at breakfast.

Inconsistent counsellor! We must take the world as we find it.

For my own part, I do not hesitate to say that I indulge in eight hours' rest every night of my life. It may be a fool's share. But I should be a greater fool if I had less. Of course, this includes the preliminary half-hours between lying down and going to sleep, and an important interval it is. All the events of the past day pass in succession through one's mind. If they include worries, disappointments, failures—if you have had a churlish answer in official life—if your dearest friend's health is failing, if your shares in the East Diddlesex have depreciated ten per cent., if your picture has been rejected at the Royal Academy, or your three-act comedy has just been 'declined with thanks,' be sure all these incidents will recur to your mind during that half-hour in the worst and most aggravating form, and in that case your journey into dreamland will be a long and tedious one. Indeed, it may be dawn before you get there.

But if you have had a tolerably successful day, heard no bad news, and worked to your satisfaction, what a delightful interval it is! You may build attractive castles in the air. You rise from obscurity to fame. The *res angusta domi* is changed by magic into wealth and comfort. You look forward to a prosperous old age, perhaps a title. There is no goal of ambition which does not seem within your reach. Life seems worth living after all, and you doze away contentedly into unconsciousness.

They tell us that after the first struggle is over the sensation of drowning is by no means unpleasant, whereas the man who is resuscitated undergoes torture. It is much the same with regard to sleep. Drowsiness has a certain charm about it. It is the waking which is so unpleasant. I don't say everywhere, but certainly in city life. To my mind, the only thing which makes it tolerable is an early cup of tea. Breakfast in bed, I think, is an over-rated joy. Children and invalids like it; to a middle-aged man it seems demoralising. But a cup of tea just brewed, hot and strong, with a dash of cream in it placed at your bedside by the maid who has just drawn aside the window curtains, and wished you a cheerful 'good morning,' what a refreshing draught of comfort it presents! It dispels that dreary feeling of *malaise* to which poor dyspeptic mortals are subject in early rising. Impending headaches fly before its genial influence. It supplements your night's rest, and nerves you for your daily labour.

I depend so much on my early cup of tea that whenever I pay my first visit to a country house, I take the hostess into my confidence overnight. I reveal my weakness and beg that it may be indulged. The request is a modest one and of course is always granted. I don't say the tea is always up to my standard in flavour, but I get it. Once, and once only, the lady (it was a relation of mine) demurred. I was quite welcome to the tea, but I was warned that it would be left at the door, not brought to my bed-side. It seems that the housemaid, a bashful creature of some forty summers, had scruples about entering the bedroom of a gentleman. Poor dear! You see she was a single woman. I often think of her and wonder whether she is married now.

Luckily, our own maid Phyllis has no such scruples. At half-past seven every morning she enters the room with my early draught, closely followed by Master 'Pixie,' who is always indulged with a saucerful of milk at the same time. He is a dog of regular habits and won't touch the milk downstairs. After he has lapped it up by my bedside he has a roll (I don't mean bread, but a tumble) on the hearth-rug, partly by way of exercise and partly with the object of wiping his moustaches. He then jumps on the bed, burrows under the eider-down until he finds a warm corner, settles himself into it and goes to sleep. Our cat Tim, a huge but good-natured creature, has on more than one occasion tried to share this privilege. But Pixie wouldn't hear of it. Tim might have the sofa, the arm-chair, the top of the mantelpiece, if he liked. But master's bed! No, that would never do. You must draw the line somewhere, as the masher remarked when he declined to visit his great-uncle.

There are no ghosts in our bedroom, and as far as I am aware, none in the house. Personally I am very glad of this, for though I have never seen a ghost, their habits of groaning, clanking chains, &c., &c., must be, by all accounts, extremely unpleasant. Nor have we ever been troubled by burglars' visits. Perhaps that is because we have not much family plate. My Aunt Tabitha certainly left me a handsome silver coffee-pot, and I believe we have a few dozen spoons and forks of the same material stowed away somewhere. Last year, too, in order to testify the high opinion in which I was held by numerous friends, and with the view of giving material expression to the respect entertained for my talents and integrity, I presented myself with a silver punch-bowl. This interesting article is deposited in a safe so impregnable to attack, that if a thief set to work on Saturday night, worked all through Sunday unobserved, with a jemmy of the latest pattern, and two pounds of the strongest blasting powder, he could hardly effect his purpose until 3 P.M. on Monday afternoon. At least so I was told by the safe manufacturer, and of course he ought to know. But as a matter of fact no such attempt has yet been made.

In old days, when, with youthful energy worthy of

a better cause, I used to sit up half the night writing for the press, I have often been disturbed by mysterious noises, which on investigation were proved to come from the adjoining house. But during one of these literary vigils, about 2 A.M., I distinctly heard what seemed to be the shutting of a door downstairs. I was alone in my study and everybody had gone to bed. What was I to do? Prudence seemed to say, 'Go to bed also and lock your door. It will be time enough to ascertain particulars to-morrow morning.'

On the other hand, it struck me, to adopt this course would be a sneaking way out of the difficulty. I considered for a moment, then lighted a candle, and holding it in my left hand, seized a poker with the other. I went down the kitchen stairs, positively whistling as I did so, but I didn't like the job at all, and I felt a peculiar tingling about the roots of my hair.

Well, I found nobody in the passage, no one in the kitchen, no one in the scullery, larder, pantry, or housekeeper's room. I opened cupboards, peered under tables and behind curtains, but found no one. Greatly relieved, I had made up my mind that it was a false alarm, and was preparing to return to my study when it occurred to me that I had not examined the housemaid's closet under the kitchen stairs. I went to it, and had no sooner turned the door handle than

M

the door itself was pushed violently outwards. . . . It was an awful moment and I was nerving myself for a deadly struggle, when a heavy portmanteau, which had been leaning against the door, fell to the ground. It had been packed by one of the servants who was to leave next day, and she had left it on a shelf from which it had slipped towards the door inside. This is the nearest approach to a burglary which I have ever experienced, but all things considered, I did not think it necessary to bring the matter under the notice of the police.

So long as a bedroom is airy and is comfortable your modern householder does not, as a rule, attach much importance to its fitting up and appearance. The lavish care which is bestowed in these days on what are called reception rooms, does not extend to the second floor. No smart 'dadoes,' elaborate friezes, delicately toned wall papers, rich tapestry, or artistic furniture surround us as we lie a-bed.

But, notwithstanding these deficiencies, the bedroom has a dignity of its own, and if there is anything in associations, it should be the most interesting apartment in the house. Within its walls, be they never so humble, we are ushered into life with all its chances for better or for worse. The first objects on which our eyes rest in this world are those contained in this room. It is here that we taste the firstfruits of a mother's love, on that bed, or may be in the cot alongside of it, we doze away the first year or two of our existence, gratifying half unconsciously our first instincts of earthly pleasure, and filling the air, Heaven knows how loudly, with an expression of our earliest grief. It is chiefly in this room that we learn to speak, to laugh, to weep, to like and dislike, to hope and fear, to suffer and to pray.

And, when all these lessons of life are learnt, when its long school-days are over and all holidays have ceased, it is still in some bedroom that most of us, sooner or later, on the completion of that period which is poetically described as a 'span,' close our weary eyes on this world for ever. We have had our run of the house in our time, but our first childhood began, and our second childhood will probably end, on the second floor.

CHAPTER VIII

IN THE BASEMENT

If I were asked what leading feature of our domestic architecture would be most likely to attract the attention of an intelligent foreigner on his first visit to the metropolis, I should unhesitatingly answer — area railings. We sons and daughters of perfidious Albion (or of merry England, if you like it better), can hardly realise ourselves the sense of extreme novelty which Mossoo must experience at finding himself in a city where he is condemned to walk or drive through endless groves of iron. Turn in what direction he will through habitable London, whether within the dingy, but eminently fashionable, purlieus of Mayfair, the spick-and-span new district of Tyburnia, Belgravia the aristocratic, Bloomsbury the respectable, Barnsbury the genteel, Clapham, Peckham, Fulham, Brompton, Hoxton, Brixton, Islington, Kensington, Kennington—north, south, east, or west—his observant eye will rest on an interminable row of cast-iron spikes.

The fact in itself is not a pleasant one to contemplate; and when Mossoo finds out that, behind these grim emblems of war, cellars are dug to a depth of some ten or twelve feet from the pavement level, in which cellars at least half the inhabitants of every house pass the greater part of their time, can't you imagine how he shrugs his shoulders, and opens his eyes with astonishment? But is it true, then, of these English, that they burrow in the ground for habitation, and condemn their domestics to reside in those *oubliettes* there? Parbleu! what a fate!

Yes; it is even so; and Mossoo knows very well that honest Jules, who brushes his clothes at home, or Babet, who, with nothing on her head but a snow-white cap, frilled to a nicety, takes his children out for a walk in the Champs Elysées, either of these good creatures, I say, would grumble roundly, even if they didn't altogether pine away under such an infliction. Whereas Sairey-Jane, who comes up from her father's cottage on Dartmoor, with a pair of rosy cheeks and a strong Devonshire accent, accommodates herself kindly to her new situation—say that of deputy sub-assistant under scullery-maid, at fifteen pounds a year and her beer—gives up the green turf and purple heather of her native soil for the prospect of a dull brick wall and coal cellar door, only enlivened by the hasty glimpse which she gets of the lower halves of passing skirts, boots, and trousers, worn by people who, from the knees upwards, are invisible to her

This is Sairey-Jane's fate, and that of Master Tom, the page, who perhaps had the run of an orchard before he bloomed into buttons; though, to be sure, he does answer the front door bell sometimes, and even goes out for an airing exactly three paces behind his 'missus,' which is so far an advantage to him.

I wonder how many of the upper ten thousand—those who live at the top, instead of the bottom of the kitchen stairs—try to realise the effect of this semi-subterraneous existence; and which of us who are placed in authority over servants, who say to one 'do this,' and he doeth it (or doesn't do it, as the case may be), which of us has explored, even in imagination, those gloomy labyrinths of the basement story? We are separated by, say, twelve inches of floor carpentry, from a little world of beings possessed of the same physical and moral sense as ourselves; with desires, hopes, fears, and digestions like our own, and we take no more count of these last than we do of the works of a watch. The use of a watch is to tell us the time; but as for the mainspring, the lever action, the double escapement, the wheels and chain, or what you will, inside, do you, my dear lady, ever trouble your head one whit regarding *them*? Of course not. How should they concern you?

Some chronometers, like that of your medical man, for instance, are made for use ; others, like that of the pretty trinket on your wrist, for ornament chiefly. So long as each serves its turn, neither you, nor Dr. Glibb, I think, will meddle with its interior. Similarly, honest John Thomas, of Bellevue Cottage, Hammersmith, who is coachman, groom, and gardener by turn, has evidently been destined by nature to make himself generally useful, while Mr. Chawles Plushington, who stands airing his calves under a certain porch in Eaton Square, may be regarded as a purely ornamental feature in your establishment. All this is the result of fate. But the private disposition of these gentlemen, the quality of their respective temperaments, the number of their brothers and sisters, and, in short, their individual circumstances out of livery, are details which, confess now, have no interest for your ladyship. Indeed, in our present advanced and highly enlightened state of civilisation, it would be unreasonable to expect otherwise.

But as a pure matter of speculation, has it ever occurred to you what these humble retainers think of *you*? Whether they may, perchance, have, over the kitchen fire, discussed *your* merits as a wife, a mother, the mistress of a household ? The notion is an extravagant one, I admit, fraught with danger to, and subversive of the first interests of good society; but, nevertheless, not altogether impossible.

You remember, no doubt, that amusing story of your nursery days about a certain Palace of Truth, in which, whoever spoke was, by an irresistible impulse, compelled to say just what he or she thought, neither more nor less. Conceive for an instant the effect of such an influence down stairs and in your presence. What would they say?—good gracious! what might they not presume to say? those cotton-velvet and bombazine-clad servitors, about those in authority over them — about you and me, for instance!

Place-aux-dames! Let us take the ladies first. There is Maria, your own maid, who, for a wage of some thirty pounds a year, laces your corset, does your back hair, selects your ball dress (taking care, of course, that you don't appear twice during the season before the same people in the same costume), alters your bonnets of February to suit the requirements of March, and insists on your ordering another befitting the month of April; who brings that fragrant cup of tea to your bedside every morning; who knows where you keep the sal-volatile and kalydor, and with whom you condescend to chat a little as she unrobes you perhaps at 2 A.M. twice a week while you stay in town.

Ah, dear, good, patient Maria — sweet-spoken and sandy-haired sycophant! cease your kindly prattle about ribbons and *rouleaux*, guipure, and Valenciennes, and tell your mistress what you really think of her. She is young, pretty, and engaging; will you dare to say she is a giddy and affected flirt? She is middle-aged, wealthy, and well born; but have you ever called her a patched-up, imperious skin-flint? I trow not. The smile with which you greet her has been assumed so long, and with such excellent effect; that rising indignation has been so studiously repressed; that unimpassioned deference has told so well in regard to vails and perquisites, that I sometimes fancy you deceive yourself among the rest of the world, and, for the time, actually imagine the middle-aged lady whom you make up for evening parties, and take to pieces just before dawn, is a model of feminine perfection.

Women, you see, are born actors, their most effective arts are so natural to them, their simplest natures often so graceful and artistic, that, from the humblest servant-maid to the most accomplished lady of the land, we can't easily distinguish—I believe that it might not be always desirable to distinguish—between what they really are and what they seem to be. In point of fact, I don't think they always know themselves.

But trusty John Thomas, and profusely powdered Chawles, only hide their spleen, their indignation and contempt, in the presence of their betters. In the butler's pantry, at the ale-house round the corner, across the hammer-cloths of their respective chariots, sentiments are expressed which neither you nor I, dear paterfamilias, could listen to unmoved. I know an old gentleman—an irascible old gentleman—who, standing by chance one afternoon inconveniently near the entrance hall of his house, after summoning his brougham for the second time that day, heard a favourite footman exclaim to the confidential valet, 'I'm blest if that darned old noosance ain't ordered out the carriage again!'

Now you know that was by no means a pleasant remark to reach one's ears in the decline of life, uttered by a paid lackey, the buttons of whose very coat were adorned with the family crest; but I am not at all sure that the old gentleman to whom I refer was justified in the severe retaliation which he adopted. The wretched Jenkins (let us call him) was dismissed on the spot, and had nothing but a month's wages to console him in his adversity. The consequence was, no doubt, that he repaired to the Black Lion that evening, and entertained his liveried friends with a very disrespectful, if not perverted account of the affair. I daresay his late master became the laughing-stock of the bar-parlour; that his wig and wizen face, his gout and gaiters, his peppery disposition and general peculiarities, were discussed in a manner which was anything but pleasant.

Now, suppose, instead of taking so summary a revenge he had retired to his study, swallowed a glass of Madeira, just to steady his nerves, rung the bell and told Jenkins not to talk so loud downstairs if he wished to keep his place. Can't you imagine how crestfallen the poor minion would have been? What an old trump the man he served must thenceforth be considered in his eyes; and with how much zeal he might have continued his service? But, 'who can be wise, amazed, temperate, and furious' as the Thane of Cawdor once justly asked, 'in a moment?' 'No man'! And upon my word, when one comes to think of it, the provocation was very great.

Personally, I must admit I have no great affection for the London flunkey of fashionable life. It is the most unfortunate stage of a man-servant's career. As a page he may be slim and interesting. As a butler he may become stout and benevolent. But a great, broad-shouldered, black-whiskered fellow of six feet, who thrusts his brawny calves into pink silk stockings, plasters his hair with flour and pomatum, and covers himself with tags and gold-lace, to hang on behind a carriage—bah! one fancies a man was made for some better business than this.

It isn't his fault, no doubt you will say. It is his betters who are to blame; they rig him up in this ridiculous costume, they set him to do this senseless work; they conduct their households on such a plan that it is difficult for him to help being what he is—mean, idle, often insolent. There are, in short, some excuses for him. And so, no doubt, a good deal may be said in favour of the wasp (black and yellow, by the way, is the orthodox colour for modern livery waistcoats), but that would not lessen the annoyance of its sting. Your ornamental footman is an institution; but the institution is a bore, and it is not exactly easy to say why it has become so.

Any of us who have conned over, or seen enacted the comedies which were written at the close of the last century, can testify to the pleasant, affable character which the stage servant of that period assumed. His master joked with him, thrashed him, confided in him, called him 'knave' and 'rascal' by turns; and yet the poor fellow not only remained in his place, but stuck by the gallant captain through thick and thin; helped him in his little intrigues, bamboozled his creditors, rushed into all sorts of risks for his sake.

Can this be said of any of our liveried retainers of

the present day? Can we imagine Jeames or Chawles conveying a *billet-doux* with the slightest interest as to its success—standing meekly to receive our blows (malacca canes have gone out of fashion now); scheming to get a dun out of the house; or even remaining a single day beneath the roof of a gentleman in urgent pecuniary difficulties? I say that type of retainer is obsolete. You can no more find it now than you can find a living specimen of the dinornis or megatherium. What! confide our *tendresses* to a fellow who blacks one's boots? Talk familiarly about debts and obligations to a man who stands behind your chair at dinner? Impossible! Why, in course of time he might take you by the button-hole and call you 'old chappie.' The present state of society no longer admits of such relations.

Women, I expect, do occasionally lapse into confidences of this kind. How otherwise could Miss Gadabout, with whose family I am tolerably intimate, have been informed of the fact that Lady Flaring has not paid her milliner's bill for the last three years; or that Cornet Spanker of the Blues had been twice refused by the wealthy widow, Mrs. Van-Chequers? These little scraps of domestic intelligence are surely picked up on the second floor, before the toilet-table, between lacing and frizzing, late nocturnal soup and early morning Pekoe.

Ah! mesdemoiselles, if you would only be a *little* more discreet with your waiting-maids! If you would only remember that that dapper little creature who 'does' your back-hair, lays out your ball-dress, selects your bracelets, ties your sash, twitches that flowing skirt into shape, hands you your gloves, and scents that little scrap of cambric and lace which you carry with such a fascinating air—if you could only bring yourself to believe that your patient, useful, clever Abigail is as great a gossip as yourself; that the harmless prattle with which you entertain her and indulge yourself, will assuredly find its way down-stairs into the servants' hall, and be carried next day to the dainty ears of a dozen of your female friends (or enemies, as the case may be), would you—could you be *quite* so frank in your revelations? Miss Papillon *is* a flirt I grant you, and the manner in which she comported herself the other night before Lord Rattlegate was very far from correct. I am quite of your opinion that, looking to Lady Screwby's position in the world, and the amount of her fortune, she ought *not* to wear cleaned gloves.

But then, my dear girls, if every detail of *your* conduct last season, if all the sacred mysteries of *your* toilet were openly discussed, which of the fairest of you would escape censure? I say nothing of Major Slingsby's attention to Miss Markham; nor of Miss Turnwell's amber-coloured silk skirt, over which that stupid footman spilt a strawberry ice last season, and which at least *some* of you recognised under a different hue this winter. I pass no comment on these things myself; I only beg of you to bear them in mind, and not to forget that what is sauce for the goose is also sauce for the gander, although I am aware that those delicious birds are not of the same sex.

It may be a morbid kind of curiosity, if you will, but I confess I do feel somewhat curious to know what forms the staple article of conversation round the kitchen-table; whether there is any standard of etiquette which regulates the social relations of this basement-story life; how much deference, for example, Mrs. Cook expects from the scullery-maid; what sort of attentions the parlour-maid may, with a due sense of propriety, receive from the butler; whether the valet patronises or only tolerates the page, and so forth.

I fancy that servants in a well-conducted household are great sticklers for decorum and the fitness of things in general. Observe the nice distinctions which they draw with regard to their respective duties, settling among themselves, by a stringent code of rules, who is to do what work. If by accident or in case of emergency the housemaid is asked to wash down the door-step, cook to lend a hand at bed-making, or John to dust his master's library, ten to one you hear of grumbling, and a talk of this or that not being his or her 'dooty.' So we may depend on it the social grades of life downstairs are jealously preserved, that the nursery-maid knows herself (as the phrase goes) better than to trespass on the prerogative of my lady's attendant, and the 'buttons' wouldn't 'go for to interfere' with Mr. John Thomas's perquisites, 'no not for nothink.'

Perquisites! Ah! then we come to a point on which I think there should be some better understanding between 'upstairs and down.' When I was a student at the Royal Academy, with a moderate allowance from the parental purse, I used to spend my Easter week at a friend's house in the country where an establishment was kept on rather a large scale. My railway journey there and back, cab fares, and other little incidental expenses, cost me on those occasions perhaps somewhat more than I was justified in spending on such an excursion. But on leaving the house a tax awaited me which I really could not afford to pay, and yet from which no young gentleman with any sense of dignity could escape.

My friend had a solemn butler—out of livery of course—with a bald head and an air of such tremendous importance that one instinctively felt (at least I did) how delicate a task it was to offer him any gratuity at all, and how utterly impossible it would have been to offer him anything less than gold without positively insulting him. The same argument applied with equal reason to the housekeeper, a demure-looking personage who had breakfast served in her own room, and whom the other servants addressed as 'mum.' Then there was my friend's valet, who condescended to bring me my shaving-water in the morning and lay out my dress-coat before dinner. There was another gentleman in livery who during that repast came frequently to me with offers of a 'little sherry, sir, little 'ock, sir,' and so forth. Finally there were the groom who brought round our horses to the door, the gardener who had always some trifle to offer in the shape of fruit or vegetables as I was leaving (no doubt they thought, or pretended to think, that I had a house and *cuisine* of my own in town, whereas I lived in Bloomsbury lodgings, and my usual dinner consisted of a couple of chops), and the lodge-keeper, who touched his hat whenever I entered or left the grounds. All these functionaries had, in turn, to be fee'd, and by the time my railway fare had been paid I was minus the best half of my last five-pound note.

Now it seems to me that this system of servant-tipping requires revision. It falls rather hard on our young friends and poor relations—guests whose purses are slender—whose wallets are not amply stored. It makes John Thomas (whose calling, as I have shown, has from other causes already degenerated) mean and calculating; it leads him to look mercenarily at every visitor to his master's house, and estimate his welcome in £ *s. d.*

There is Freeman's housemaid, for instance, who used to smile and drop me the neatest little curtsies you ever saw whenever I called on her master. The angelic behaviour of that girl, the modest neatness of her white aprons, the tidy coquetry of her caps, the arch simplicity of her manner—she was only nineteen—completely won my heart. I don't mind admitting it now, for she has been married for some years to the grocer's young man, and they have since set up in that line for themselves. Well, in an evil moment I—don't be frightened, ladies, I have the very strictest sense of propriety—I took to giving this young woman small gratuities: for example, when she occasionally helped me on with my greatcoat, a shilling; when she called a cab for me, a florin; when she took charge of my Scotch terrier in the kitchen (Mrs. F. couldn't bear dogs), half-a-crown, and so forth.

One day my host found me out in my well-meant indiscretion, and being of an eccentric turn of humour rated me in his own ironical way. 'My dear fellow,' said he, 'don't let me see you do that again. I pay that girl ample wages; if they are not high enough she can ask for more, and if she deserves it she shall have them. But meanwhile I don't see why, as my guest, you should contribute to her support. If you think your entertainment here deserves some recognition, you may present me, at the close of every year, with a gold pencil-case, or what you will. Personally, I should hardly consider any such *honorarium* necessary, but please don't demoralise my servants by tipping them.

The result of this tremendous chaff (the drift of which I well understood, for Freeman's own generosity knew no bounds) was that Miss Harriet's half-crowns were cut off, at least as far as I was concerned. Except at Christmas--which, you know, only comes once a year, and, regarded purely from a financial point of view, once is quite enough, in my opinion—that bewitching creature did not add sixpence more to her wages out of my pocket.

It may have been owing to her master's cruel interference with her perquisites in this and other instances that she united herself at a month's warning with Mr. Spicely; or it may have been that youth's ardent devotion which caused her to take so precipitate a step. On that point it is not necessary for me to record an opinion. All I know is that I had from that day forth no more smiles, no more curtsies, no more inquiries after the health of my skye-terrier. I called my own cabs, pulled on my own greatcoat, shut the front door in Grosvenor Street with my own hands, and have been very suspicious of ancillary blandishments ever since.

There are two sides, however, to every question, and lest I should for an instant be supposed to defend stinginess to servants, let me here protest that I consider no kind of shabbiness more mean, no frugality more ill-advised, no providence more wasteful than that which in any household is enjoined alone downstairs. 'A fat kitchen and a lean parlour' was a homely proverb once in vogue, and certainly, if both cannot be well fed, it must be a miserable sort of thriftiness which would begin by starving the basement story. Yet I have heard of respectable, well-bred housewives who ration their servants like union paupers, who cut down their daily food to a minimum, who consider a half-pint of small beer an amply sufficient stimulant for an able-bodied, hard-working cook, and who regard the bare mention of meat suppers in the kitchen as flat heresy.

There is something half-ludicrous, half-contemptible in this penny-wise economy. Upstairs and before her guests we have madame doing the honours of her table—a table crowded with needless delicacies

—soups, entremets, game, pâtés, dessert, delicately *named* wines (I say nothing of the quality), and what not. Could we foresee our hostess as she will probably appear next morning, marshalling the fragments of this gorgeous banquet in her bleak larder, taking stock of half-consumed chicken and segments of raised pie, counting the forcemeat balls which adorned that dish of jugged hare, noting with a scrupulous eye the mortal remains of a beloved turkey, which of us would enjoy his dinner?

Such relics may indeed worthily supply the family table for some days to come, but while all this feasting has been going on upstairs, how have the servants fared? 'What! *that* all of the shoulder of mutton which was ordered so recently? Impossible! Those custards eaten because they wouldn't keep another day? Absurd! I am convinced that the best part of a pheasant, and *not* a drumstick only, was sent down last night, and what presumption to eat game in the kitchen!'

Ah, my dear *materfamilias*, would you muzzle the ox that treadeth out the corn? Enough may not be always as good as a feast, but let us, at least, have enough in the servants' hall before we attempt feasting in the dining-room. The reverse of this rule represents not only a moral wrong but a financial mistake. Hungry servants must eat, whether they confess to the weakness or not. A good slice off the joint will satisfy their appetites as well as a series of oyster-patties, but if they are debarred from the first, can you be surprised at their making free with the other?

Good servants, who wish (in downstair language) to 'better themselves,' and who want a fair character for their next place, never protest against these petty exactions. Besides, the icy reserve and conventional propriety which is kept up (perhaps necessarily in this country) between man and master, maid and mistress, make it impossible to do so openly. But if this traditional gag were just for a day removed from the lips of honest John Thomas and Betsy Jane, my goodness! what a shout of derision would rise from the areas of Mayfair; with what loud bursts of vulgar indignation Belgravian basements would ring!

There is not unfrequently in 'high life' a great deal which might be contemplated with advantage by philosophers below stairs. Do the philosophers avail themselves of this teaching? I fear not. Jeames and Chawles, Susan and Betty, imitate the foibles no less than the virtues of their betters. We all admit and deplore that spirit of flunkeydom which pervades certain phases of English society, which sets half our dear fellow-countrymen truckling to a man who has a handle to his name, or, worse still, to another who is known to possess a large fortune. After this, can you sneer at the mixture of sham deference and twopenny dignity of the servant who wears, for your sake, a cockade, tags, powder, and heraldic buttons?

I think it is a mistake to suppose that servants despise and chafe under these insignia of office. My own opinion is, that if livery went out of fashion for footmen, butlers would at once petition to wear it. A due and palpable distinction between the two places must be kept up, or the kitchen would be in a state of anarchy. What! a drab coat or a striped vest the badge of slavery? The badge of fiddlesticks! A domestic servant is not more rigidly tied to his duties than a soldier, or a government office clerk, or a barrister, or a poor curate, who is often harder worked than a London footman, and not nearly so well remunerated. We don't call a scarlet coat, or a horsehair-wig, or a stuff gown the badge of slavery; why should an honest suit of livery be so stigmatised? Prate as they will about their free-born rights and privileges, servants are the first to respect these relics of ancient feudalism.

CHAPTER IX

OUR AMUSEMENTS

It is happily ordained by Fate that a man's sense of pleasure is sure to vary sooner or later with his time of life. I say sooner or later, because it is really wonderful how some of us retain in middle age, and even afterwards, certain tastes and forms of enjoyment which one might naturally suppose would have been long survived. There are popular prints and pictures representing the enthusiastic but gouty angler, dangling his rod and fly over a big washing-tub, or an old gentleman of the last century propped up in his bed and looking on, with bleared eyes, at a cockfight. But these we must, I think, admit are exceptions to the rule.

Boyhood, youth, man's estate, and the period of fogeydom are each in turn associated with their own appropriate hobbies and pursuits, and just as we turn with impatience from the beardless prig who assumes the experience of his grandsire, so the sight of an ancient dame *décolletée* and bedecked with diamonds, sitting at a dinner party when she ought to have exchanged her *toupet* for an honest night-cap and to have been comfortably abed at home, inspires the reflective observer with dismay.

I perfectly well remember the time (it seems, as we figuratively say, but yesterday) when a visit to Madame Tussaud's Exhibition, or the Zoological Gardens, or, better still, to a pantomime at Covent Garden, seemed in my unsophisticated judgment to realise an ideal of human bliss. A little later to score a dozen runs in a school cricket match, to sail 'half-deckers' in Chelsea Reach, or to secure the hand of Miss Polkington at a little 'hop' in Harley Street, gave me a sensation of genuine happiness.

Well, I must confess that in maturer years these joys, together with many others, have lost their zest. They have been succeeded by new tastes, fresh kinds of pleasure, the product perhaps of experience, mental discipline, ambition, love of work, or what you will. Anyhow, a change has occurred, and I don't care now for what I enjoyed twenty years ago.

For instance, public dinners bore me. I have swallowed enough turtle soup to last me for life, and if I were told that I should never taste calipee or calipash again in this world, I should bear my fate with equanimity. Punch *à la Romaine* has lost its charm. Whitebait seems to me a much overrated delicacy. My eyes are no longer dazzled by the splendour of city plate. Even the ceremony of the loving-cup, especially when I stand up to pledge a fellow-guest with luxuriant moustaches, appears not unattended with drawbacks.

I am one of the most loyal subjects in Her Majesty's dominions, but I don't care to hear common-place remarks about the Royal Family made in so perfunctory a manner, that one requires a bumper of Lafite to wash down the dry toast. Oh! those after-dinner speeches: the Army and Navy—their exploits on shore and their prowess afloat; the improvements in modern armaments; the wooden walls of old England represented by ironclads and torpedo-boats [for your modern admiral is generally a theorist, and not unfrequently treats his audience to an impromptu lecture on naval construction]; the urgent necessity for increasing our fleet; defence, not defiance; the excellent tone and unquestionable utility of our subsidiary forces; winding up with the novel sentiment that England expects every man to do his duty—have we not all listened in turn to this patriotic if inexpensive rhetoric for half-an-hour at a stretch, and blessed our stars when the knife handles rattling on the table proclaimed the fact that the orator had resumed his seat?

Perhaps the Nawab of Rum-ti-foo (a coloured gentleman with peculiar notions on the subject of diet) finds his name associated with 'Our Foreign Allies,' or the Hon. Chiltern Centums, M.P., rising to return thanks for the House of Commons, begins by admitting that in such a mixed assembly as he sees before him, the field of politics is delicate ground, and forthwith proceeds to air his views on protection, let us say—or manhood suffrage.

As for art, science, and literature, their respective representatives occupy at least an hour longer in talking about them, sometimes in a vein which suggests that they had only been discovered last week and required a lengthy apology for existence.

When will men learn that the secret of any after-dinner speech is to make it short, epigrammatic, and cheerful? I say 'cheerful,' because we are not al wits, and it is not given to every orator to raise a laugh, even after his fair share of Clicquot. But at least he need not be lugubrious or launch into platitudes. Anyhow he can keep an eye on his watch.

No, I don't like public dinners. As a rule they are not graced by the presence of ladies, conversation with whom promotes digestion, and enables a man to decline every alternate *entrée*. In their absence we eat and drink too much; we get bored to death with long perorations. And then comes the next morning, bringing with it post-prandial remorse and, perhaps, a bilious headache.

Next to a public dinner, perhaps the 'Private View' of a picture exhibition may be regarded as the most delusive joy of modern life. Of course, there are exhibitions and exhibitions. One or two which I will not presume to name are better managed than others. But speaking generally, and of the form which such entertainments have assumed within the last ten years or so, it must be confessed that the time spent in attending these functions cannot exactly be described as *horæ serenæ*.

In the first place I object to the word 'private' being used to designate a throng. As a rule your private view day is the most crowded one in the year. If you are waiting outside when the doors open you may have a chance of seeing a few pictures. But if you arrive after lunch you will probably have to elbow your way up a staircase closely packed with your fellow-creatures—squeezing, struggling, panting amateurs, whose physical condition when they *do* reach the galleries above, is such as to demoralise an athlete, to say nothing of æsthetes. You are jostled to and fro, turned round like a teetotum, shake hands with friends over somebody else's shoulder, find every seat occupied, and if, in the course of time, you succeed in getting in front of a picture, you are so hemmed in by the crowd that you have a difficulty in keeping your nose off the canvas. If, in despair, you take refuge in the refreshment room, you will have to pay sixpence for a cup of the most detestable infusion which was ever offered to exhausted mortals under the name of tea.

And then the company by which you are surrounded! I am not an over-fastidious man. I ride in twopenny omnibuses, and, before now, have made myself pleasant to bagmen in the bar-parlour of a rustic inn. But a private view, the invitations to which are presumably issued to the *élite* of the art world, and where, nevertheless, you meet as queer a lot of people as on a Bank Holiday at the Crystal Palace, I must say puzzles me. I feel honoured by the compliment of a card, but I prefer to wait for a week or so, pay my shilling like a man, and see the pictures in comfort.

Garden-parties are pleasant enough, especially if the weather is fine, the hostess genial, and the grounds are pretty. Here, at least, you are in fresh air, and as there is plenty of space you can move from group to group and join the friends you like best, which is not always possible in a London drawing-room. The entertainment, too, admits of a greater variety of costume, not only for the ladies—bless their decorative instincts!—but for men, who, escaping from the black broadcloth which modern Fashion, with an impartial hand, has prescribed alike for funerals and evening parties, can attire themselves in delicate shades of grey or brown, indulge their fancy in the hue of trousers, or blossom out in ties and scarves of unusual gaiety.

If the grounds are extensive, and cool retreats, *sub tegmine fagi*, are accessible, the opportunities afforded to young people of pairing off are inestimable. Prudent mammas and lynx-eyed chaperons relax their vigilance at a garden-party. Nor do I think, as a perfectly impartial and disinterested fogey, that they need feel much uneasiness on that score. In these days it seems to me that, so far as polite society is concerned, the rising generation of both sexes can be safely trusted to take care of themselves. My lady 'sweet and twenty,' nowadays, with all her charming artlessness, is not the giddy, impulsive creature described in novels of a bygone age. She is often a girl of what is called culture, not much given to romance, and generally takes a practical view of life.

As for the modern 'masher,' if one may judge from his appearance, he is at pains to eliminate from his expression every spark of emotion. He suppresses his feelings (we will assume that he has some at times) so successfully that I defy you to guess when he is pleased and when he is not. His rigid unsympathetic look is a sort of negation of individuality. The only parallel type in creation with which I am familiar is the countenance of a coachman on a private brougham, who considers it bad form to turn his head to the right or left, lest he should betray an interest in anything but his horse.

No, there is not much danger in the social intercourse of this nineteenth-century youth, this *fin-de-siècle* miss. A little discreet flirtation, if you please, but no imprudence. They are both too wide awake. She is not likely to bestow her young affections on a struggling author, an unknown artist, a briefless barrister, or indeed on any man who is not in a position to give her a well-appointed home. While he, who appreciates the luxury of his club and lives well up to his income, is in no hurry to sacrifice the freedom of bachelor life for a marriage which does not bring with it some assurance of financial prospects. Elopements are very rare in our time. The telegraphic wire may have something to do with it, but if we read between the lines—the marriage lines, I mean—we shall find inscribed in a legible hand the letters £ *s. d.*, which, I think, represent a still more deterrent influence.

Having no technical knowledge of music, my relish for that art is, I confess, mainly confined to *tunes*, for which, they tell me, I have an accurate ear and retentive memory. But in this Wagnerian age tunes count for nothing. Handel I enjoy, as it were, by accident, and being quite unable to explain why or wherefore, I feel that it is a sort of presumption on my part to aspire to such exalted pleasure. But Bach's fugues are too much for me. I sit like a dunce listening to a language which is unintelligible.

In the days of my youth, when Grisi and Mario were still popular favourites, I went to the Opera like the rest of the world, and I have never forgotten the old familiar airs in 'Norma,' 'La Sonnambula,' 'Masaniello,' 'Il Barbiere, 'Fra Diavolo,' 'Don Giovanni,' 'I Puritani,' 'Marta,' 'Der Freischütz,' the 'Huguenots,' and a dozen other productions which are no more likely to reappear now than the Cock Lane Ghost. Verdi, Rossini, Donizetti, and Meyerbeer are out of date. We have grown too scientific—too philosophical—for their inventions.

Consequently, when the De Majors bid us to one of their choice recital evenings, I let my wife go alone. She enjoys this sort of thing and it would be selfish to deprive her of a harmless pastime. But when I am present at a private concert—when I look round and see the expressions of my fellow-guests, all, so to speak, wrapped in an agony of bliss, when I know that piece will succeed piece, and movement follow movement, andante, allegro, pizzicato, and all the rest of it—with five minutes' interval for conversation, and a half melted strawberry ice to keep one's spirits up—why, I feel that I am intruding, that I ought to be ashamed of myself for taking up so much room, and that it would be better for me to be at home with an evening paper and my pipe!

There is perhaps no form of amusement which in my time I have enjoyed so long and so thoroughly as that afforded by the stage. I was taken to a theatre for the first time at the age of eight. It was an epoch in my life. To this day I have never forgotten the rapture of excitement into which I was thrown by everything that I heard and saw. The orchestral music, the brilliant gas-lights, the gilded decorations of the proscenium surmounted by a large bas-relief representing a white swan (emblematical of the Bard of Avon); the drop scene—probably a third-rate work of art, for we were in a provincial town; the tinkling bell which rang before the curtain rose, and the enchanting scene which revealed itself a few moments later, all filled me with unutterable delight. The performance was a pantomime, preceded of course by a fairy tale, with which I was familiar. The princess appeared to me a model of feminine beauty, with a faultless complexion (I had never heard of rouge). Puss in Boots was irresistibly comical—only I thought him on too large a scale—and as for Harlequin's tricks they seemed positively miraculous.

Ten years later I wanted, like many other foolish

boys, to be an actor myself. I constantly took part in private theatricals, and have often since wondered at my temerity and the patience of my audiences. But in those days if a young fellow took to the stage as a profession, he had, practically, to take leave of his old friends, often to be dropped by his own family. Well, *nous avons changé tout cela*, and perhaps have gone too far in the opposite extreme. I don't suppose there ever was a time when actors and actresses were so fêted, caressed, and welcomed by smart society as at the present day. It is enough to turn their heads.

A kindly fate ordained that instead of appearing on what used to be called 'the boards' (every stage floor is carpeted now) I should take my seat modestly on the other side of the curtain, and for many years of my life I have occupied it at intervals with immense satisfaction. Shades of Kean, Phelps, and Wallack, of Farren, Alfred Wigan, and dear old Charley Mathews, facetious Harley, roguish Buckstone, drily-comical Keeley, if you still haunt the scenes of your former triumphs, I hope you will recognise the writer of these lines as one of your many admirers.

I should like to ask Wright's ghost if he remembered once winking at me distinctly in a private box, and hear portly Paul Bedford (who must surely be with him still) shout back an assuring response, 'I believe you, my b-hoy'!

Three only, out of a host of charming actresses whom I remembered in those days are still living. The rest have vanished in company with Mesdames Nisbet, Reynolds, Horton, Woolgar, Celeste, and other dramatic angels, and with their departure a great change has come over the British stage. Shakespeare indeed is from time to time played at one or two houses. But where are the brilliant comedies of Sheridan, the romantic dramas of Lord Lytton, the ingenious inventions of Tom Taylor, the wholesome, witty, and thoroughly home-spun plays of Robertson?

The jaded appetite of a modern British audience is not satisfied with this simple fare. It has been spoilt by French dishes, and we periodically crave for something more and still more spicy. The latest piece which has found popularity in Paris is produced in a translated form, adapted or imitated more or less successfully for our benefit.

If it includes an intrigue, or a seduction, a forgery or a murder, so much the better, provided, of course, that the author takes care to make his criminal interesting. We are shocked at all this wickedness, but then the play is supposed to hold the mirror up to nature: it points such an excellent moral, and besides, the part of Mrs. Bolsover is played by such an accomplished *artiste*.

Well, I confess I have no taste for this sort of performance. It is all very well for the young ladies who, I am told, are allowed to enjoy it, but I should not feel comfortable to sit through such a piece in their company. I am too old a sinner to suppose that it would demoralise *me*, but I know that I should come away with an unpleasant sensation. When I go to a play I like to be either amused or edified. Of the two I prefer to be amused. But I don't want to be horrified. Partly on this account and partly because we live at least three miles from the nearest theatre, I don't attend plays so often as I used to.

There is one form of amusement in which we have indulged for many years past, and which, recurring as it does but annually, does not pall upon any but a jaded taste. The man who is doomed to pass ten out of every twelve months in London must be blasé indeed if he cannot enjoy a six weeks' trip on the Continent. I don't say that it is without its drawbacks. In the first place the penalty which awaits some of us in crossing the Channel is a severe one to those who, like your humble servant, suffer excruciatingly from what is politely called *mal de mer*. It is all very well to laugh at it. To me it is no joking matter, and I am grateful that I live in days when the progress of science has reduced the passage time in fair weather to ninety minutes, for I often feel that ten minutes more would render my return ticket useless. Indeed, on one occasion I suffered so much prostration in mind and body that I inwardly resolved never to return to England again unless the Channel Tunnel Bill passed in Parliament, and there was a reasonable prospect of the work being completed, say, in ten years.

When I add that in order to avoid crossing the North Sea we once went to Norway by way of Cologne, you may conclude that I am in earnest. It seems a roundabout route, to be sure, but if you consult the pages of Bradshaw, you will find that, supposing one is a bad sailor, with plenty of time to spare, this overland journey can be accomplished. You go from Calais to Aix-la-Chapelle, thence to Cologne and Hamburg; cross salt but land-locked water between Fredericia and Strib, Nyborg and Korsœr, and so on viâ Copenhagen to Christiania, drive across country, and there you are.

But this is digression in more senses than one. My present remarks relate to the Continent, and it may be frankly admitted that although journeys there are cheaper and speedier than they used to be, travelling abroad in some respects is not so pleasant as it used to be. The manners of railway guards and porters have deteriorated. The quality of food at station buffets (always excepting at Goschenen on the St. Gothard line, which is faultless) cannot be called satisfactory. I don't like to pay fifteen francs a night for a fourth floor bedroom in a smart hotel at Lucerne, when I remember that not many years ago a third of that sum would have been considered an exorbitant charge.

To be conveyed in an omnibus lighted by electricity up to the doors of a palatial establishment at Zürich and get scarcely enough to eat at the table d'hôte, involves an inconsistency which I am unable to explain. Personally I would rather have less splendour and more comfort. It is irritating to find that even at Bordeaux mine host supplies his guests with 'ordinaire' at four francs a bottle which could only have cost him eight sous. When I retire to rest I prefer an extinguisher for my candle to the nuisance of blowing it out and leaving the room redolent of tallow, more especially as my bill the next morning retains the fiction (and the price) of two wax bougies. And as the same document is supposed to include a fair remuneration for service, I object to see waiters and femmes de chambre loitering about in expectation of a fee.

Freeborn Britons who believe in the liberty of the subject resent being cooped up in the waiting-room of a continental railway station until their train runs in, when, hampered with small baggage, they have to rush out and struggle for a seat. '*En voiture!*' is an aggravating cry when one knows from experience that ten minutes will certainly elapse before the train starts. We must confess that Continental railway carriages, once so superior to our own, have not kept pace with the times in regard to comfort, and that an English porter will do more expeditiously for sixpence that for which a *träger* or a *facchino* (when you can catch him) often demands two francs.

These and a hundred other petty inconveniences await the British tourist who spends his holiday abroad instead of in his own country. But after a large experience of both I do not hesitate to prefer the Continent. It is more of a change. I have tried sea-side places on our own beloved coast. I have tried Scotland, Yorkshire, Derbyshire, and Devonshire. I have made expeditions to North Wales and the Cumberland Lakes. I delight in the scenery of our own dear island, and on the whole I like the manners of its natives far better than those of 'them foreign chaps.' But somehow the latter beat us hollow in the art of hotel keeping. And what is more, you meet better company abroad. In these days, of course, snobs travel everywhere, but I will say this, that among your fellow tourists in Germany, France, Switzerland, or Italy, there is generally a good range of choice.

In this country it is not so. At a British watering-place there must be, of course, now and then agreeable and well-bred people. But as a rule they keep to themselves, dine alone, and ten to one have a private sitting-room which keeps them apart from their fellow tourists. On the Continent alone do they shake off that freezing insular reserve which at home makes hotel society impossible. A table d'hôte and public drawing-room may be fraught with terrors to the exclusive, but sensible mortals do not neglect an opportunity for agreeable intercourse.

For instance, I owe many pleasant friendships to Switzerland. We have stayed at nearly every place of popular resort in that cheerful and health-giving country. I can find my way about Bernė and Geneva, Basel and Lucerne, better than in any provincial town of England. I have no head for climbing, but I can manage my twenty or thirty miles afoot. I have walked over the Furca and Grimsel, and tramped through the whole length of the Engadine Valley from Samaden to Maloja. I know every pass accessible on wheels, I have spent weeks in sketching on the Lake of Thun. I have been snowed up at Mürren, and consorted with members of the Alpine Club at Zermatt.

I look with wonder at these British athletes returning with guides, ropes, and ice-axes from their various expeditions. I listen to them as they tell us how they 'did' this or that 'horn' in so many hours, and I wonder sometimes whether they really enjoyed the mountain scenery more than I, who looked at it humbly over a smiling cornfield in the valley. I am ashamed to confess in the presence of such hardy mountaineers that I never ascended anything higher than the Gorner Grat, and that my nearest approach to Mont Blanc was the Pavillon de la Pierre Pointue. As for the Matterhorn, the very idea of scaling it fills me with dismay, although I am aware that some enterprising Englishwomen were once hauled to the summit. Glaciers have no charm for me, especially when there are crevasses about, and I feel uncomfortable even in an ice-cavern.

Thank goodness there are plenty of spots in Switzerland where one can get bracing air, fine scenery, and healthy exercise without risking one's neck to look at nature. I enjoy a walk over the Via Mala and the Julier Alp, but you cannot be always on the tramp. As to resting-places, mountain hotels, and villages I could name a dozen in the Bernese Oberland, the Valais, and the Grisons where we have from time to time spent a fortnight or so to our great satisfaction.

There is Rosenlaui, with its green pastures and charming woodland; Evolena, which you reach from the Rhone valley, rich in picturesque old chalets and peopled with a stalwart, well-to-do peasantry, whose costume suggests a mediæval tradition; Champéry, where window gardening reaches the level of a fine art; Maderanerthal, into whose lovely valley a dozen waterfalls descend; Vevey, with its quaint old town and hospitable Hotel Monnet on the shore of Lake Leman; Axenfels and Axenstein, perched high above the broad blue waters of Luzernersee; Engelberg, in its green plain; Wiesen, on the sunny slope of the Rothhornstock, where the village seems at least two hundred years old, and where you may find a fresh walk every day for a month; romantic Riederalp, bustling Ragatz, Teutonicised St. Moritz, and half cockneyfied Chamonix. I know them all, and could, if I chose, describe their several characteristics or attractions. But considering that many of these places are familiar to many of my readers, and in view of the fact that information of this kind is afforded in a far more useful form by Murray and Baedeker, I refrain from details.

In this blasé age it has somehow become the fashion to despise Switzerland as too hackneyed a resort for holiday folks. It is a passing folly, for the great playground of Europe has a host of attractive districts still unexplored by the ordinary tourist. And when the weather becomes too chilly for mountain hotels, what is easier—thanks to the skill of its great engineer, than to pass over by the St. Gothard line into sunny Italy. Even if you only keep to the Lake districts, what a host of lovely resting-places attract you on the other side of the Alps! Como, Bellaggio, Cadenabbia, Baveno, Locarno, Orta, Lugano—the only difficulty lies in making a choice.

Or you may go further and visit gay, bustling Milan—escape from the heat of the day into the grateful shade of its Cathedral aisles, or spend a few delightful hours in the Brera and Ambrosian Library studying the pictures in those famous collections. Verona, Bergamo, Brescia, and a host of North Italian towns contain untold treasures of art which, I fancy, one examines with fresh zest after rusticating awhile in rugged Switzerland or the peaceful Tyrol.

As for Venice, I have seen it in all seasons except the depth of winter, and I can truly say that after all our wanderings in Europe that wonderful city of islands stands apart in my memory as the fairest, the most romantic, and the most interesting store-house of human art that I have ever explored. There is nothing like it in the world. Even Mr. Ruskin's fascinating three volumes, which I read in my teens, failed to prepare me for its unique beauty, its unequalled splendour.

To this day, and although I know it is architectural heresy to say so—its venerable Duomo, gay even in its old age—pleases me more than any cathedral that I ever entered. I have examined the contents of nearly every picture gallery on the Continent, but I come back with renewed pleasure to the dear old Accademia, rich as it is in a school of art unrivalled, to my mind, by any other in the evolution of national taste.

Florence and Rome are too far afield for brief holiday trips, but I have spent the best part of a winter in each city, years ago, and if the fates are propitious I hope to re-visit them some day. Florence, when I last saw it, had not changed so much as one might have expected. Perhaps the accident of its being no longer a Royal capital has tended as much as anything to preserve its structural integrity. As for Rome, an old friend who remembers it in the picturesque age of Papal rule, told me not long ago that he scarcely knew it again after an interval of twenty years, and that he sometimes fancied himself in Tyburnia !

It is manifestly unfair to judge of any town from a short visit, but when I find myself in Germany I always feel that I must be on my good behaviour. In Berlin, for instance, where there is much to respect and not a little to admire, I am struck by the stern officialism of the place. Even the station-master is an autocrat, and the military gentlemen look like scientific professors masquerading in uniform. I am downright afraid of the native police. At Dresden, where you may profitably spend a fortnight in the Royal Gallery, another in the Historical Museum, and a third in the Green Vault, devoting your evenings to the most delightful smoking concerts, supplied with the best music and the purest beer that the art of man has yet devised, I was once called seriously to account for walking on the wrong side of a bridge.

Sometimes we have stayed at pleasant Munich on our road to Oberammergau and the Bavarian Highlands, or found our way to the Salz Kammergut and divided our time between Salzburg, Gmunden, and Berchtesgaden. In one eventful year we disported ourselves in the Pyrenees, and then went on to Madrid. Travelling, in short, is one of our chief amusements. The time may come when, like other pleasures, it will pall, or when with advancing age one may shrink from the fatigue of long railway journeys, the bustle of hotel life, the trouble of sight-seeing. It is only in anticipation of that remote period that I find apology for the nearly obsolete practice of keeping a diary.

CHAPTER X

OUR CIRCLE

In the days of my boyhood I read with admiration and the aid of a Latin dictionary, Cicero's famous essay 'De Amicitiâ.' The form in which it is presented to the reader led me to wonder—such is the simplicity of youth—how that distinguished orator and philosopher could have remembered with so much accuracy, not only the lecture delivered by Lælius to his sons-in-law after the death of Scipio Africanus, but even the remarks with which his discourse was interrupted by Fannius and Scævola, whose neatly turned sentences serve to elicit further eloquence and wisdom from their gifted master.

To my irreverent and as yet undisciplined mind, those two deferential gentlemen somewhat resembled Masters Sandford and Merton, sitting under the tuition of Dr. Barlow, and as, with the experience gained by increasing years, the utterances of that cultured divine and pedagogue seemed to me not altogether devoid of affectation, so some of the sentiments expressed by the eminent sage and consul appear rather stilted and artificial in quality. In the first place, he sets out with the notion that friendship can only exist between men who are themselves models of perfection.

> 'Sed hoc primum sentio, nisi in bonis amicitiam esse non posse : . . . . nec sine virtute amicitia esse ullo pacto potest.'

This is rather a bad look-out for some of us weak, erring mortals, who would soon be cast adrift in the world if our friends turned their backs upon us on the first discovery of a fault.

Damon, who is a free-handed fellow, occasionally overdraws his banker's account, which is reprehensible. Pythias, who keeps well within his income, often loses his temper at trifles. Jones, a most amiable mortal, lies abed of a morning when he ought to be at his desk in the city. His old pal and schoolfellow Robinson is the soul of industry, but it must be confessed that he sometimes takes too much claret after dinner. Are these gentlemen respectively to cut each other because of their foibles?

Again, according to Lælius, friendship may be defined as a perfect unanimity of opinions on religious and social questions combined with the highest degree of mutual esteem and affection.

> 'Est autem amicitia nihil aliud, nisi omnium divinarum humanarumque rerum cum benevolentiâ et caritate summâ consensio.'

What! can there be no cordial intercourse between Tom Chasuble who is a Ritualist, and Jack Broadley who believes in evolution? Don't we all know a dozen instances of men who sit on opposite benches in the House of Commons and yet in private life meet each other on terms of mutual esteem, good fellowship, and social loyalty?

A little Utopian too, and opposed to modern experience, are the old philosopher's remarks that men ought not to be drawn towards each other by the hope of mutual aid or a sense of their own deficiencies. Surely many a well-intentioned but nervous and vacillating mortal has derived strength and encouragement from advice supplied by the more robust and energetic character of his chum. If we are not to expect or to receive benefits from those who like us, from whom shall we get them? and what becomes of the old English saw, that 'a friend in need is a friend indeed'?

Lælius believes that the better opinion a man has of himself, the better friend he is likely to prove. Well, if that was true nearly two thousand years ago, the sentiment sounds a little priggish in the nineteenth century. But there are passages in this conversational lecture which will be everlastingly wise, and which appeal to every man whose heart is not warped by misanthropy. For instance:

'Quis potest esse vita vitalis, qui non in amici mutuâ benevolentiâ conquiescat? Quid dulcius quam habere quocum omnia audeas sic loqui ut tecum?' &c., &c.

What would life be indeed without a friend, and how on earth should we get through it without someone willing to share our tastes, congratulate us on our last bit of good luck, or listen to our grievances?

Sometimes the opinions expressed in the essay reach us as it were third hand. Cicero narrates what Lælius said and Lælius recollects an observation made to him by Scipio; but there is no doubt respecting the truth of one of these traditional utterances, viz., that 'nothing is more difficult than to preserve through life an uninterrupted friendship,' and a rather melancholy reflection it is.

The intimacies which exist between schoolboys are often blotted out even during the few years passed at Oxford or Cambridge. Dick and Harry are sworn friends at college, but somehow they drift apart after leaving their *alma mater*. New tastes are formed, fresh influences operate. A disparity of means or social position such as we never suspected in the sixth form reveals itself during university life, and later on draws Dick into the world of London fashion, or consigns Harry to his rural vicarage. It takes a few years more to discover that the lucky prizeman from whom we expected so much is often but a dull

P

fellow after all, while the poor wretch who with difficulty scrambled through a pass degree may, as time goes on, win reputation as a dashing soldier or adroit diplomatist.

What has success in life to do with friendship? 'Nothing,' the man of heart would say. 'I don't care whether my old crony Goodenough is a brilliant man or not. What does it matter to me whether he can write Q.C. after his name, or whether he is still eking out a livelihood as a grey-haired junior?—whether he wears a rosette in his hatband and assumes the title of very reverend, or owns a paltry living of 300*l.* a year?—whether he has been elected a member of the Royal Academy, or is still painting pot boilers to support his family? To me he is, and always will be, the same dear old Goodenough of twenty years ago. Position be hanged! I mean to stick by him and shall do so to the end of my days.'

The man of the world thinks differently. To him it is a matter of paramount importance whether the friend of his youth holds a social position equal to his own. Goodenough courted and prosperous, Goodenough whom everybody knows, the eminent physician, the brilliant member, or the popular author, is worth remembering. A score of invitations deck the mantelpiece of his library; a dozen friends are ready to greet him at the club; no social entertainment is complete without him. But if fortune has dealt hardly with our old acquaintance, if he is wanting in the tact, the energy, the talents, or the opportunity to win his spurs in the battle of life, well of course we are sorry for him, and all that, but how can we keep up acquaintance with a nobody, or find our way to his house in Camden Town?

Sometimes the fault is not always on one side. Taking the average social unit in London for instance, I should say that a tolerable amount of success in life is generally attended by a certain loss of some old friends who, prompted by a queer, undefinable feeling, I won't call it jealousy, keep aloof from a man whose luck has been greater than their own. They banter him about his comparative prosperity, pretend to suppose that as he has got on in the world he won't remember old days or care to keep up their acquaintance, whereas the truth is that they don't care to retain his own.

What is the remedy for this cause of estrangement?

'Ut igitur,' says Lælius, 'ii qui sunt in amicitiâ conjunctionisque necessitudine superiores, exæquare se cum inferioribus debent: sic inferiores dolere non debent, se a suis amicis aut ingenio, aut fortunâ, aut dignitate superari,' &c.

Yes, that is the real secret of retaining friendship between those who are separated one from another by disparity of intellect, of social station, or of worldly means. Why should a man with big brains regard himself as a more exalted personage than his old schoolfellow who has a capacious heart? From a material point of view, both are physical organs, often owing their magnitude, substance, or quality to inherited nature, the temperament of your nursemaid, the character of your education, even sometimes to the balance at your father's bankers.

A sensible man who stands six feet three in his stockings does not give himself airs on account of his height. Why should another, the girth of whose cranium exceeds by a few inches the average size, carry it more proudly on that account? A genius has no more right to give himself airs than a philanthropist, and indeed not so much. But when we find either of them prating about culture or benevolence we may fairly suspect that one is a humbug and the other a prig.

By this time the honest reader, especially if he should be of an inquisitive turn of mind, will perhaps expect from the title of this chapter that I am going to describe the social habits, disposition, and character of some of my personal friends. Indeed, nothing would be easier than to fill these pages with reminiscences of men and women whom I have known. I might sketch their portraits in pen and ink to the life, laud their virtues, moralise over their failings, make fun of their peculiarities, and detail a vast deal of gossip, more or less amusing, respecting not only their own lives but those of their families, their uncles, aunts, cousins, and so forth.

Unless I am much mistaken, a large proportion of your modern society novels consists of such descriptions, which are read with relish, especially if the people referred to are familiar figures in the London world, and can be recognised under the thin disguise of a pseudonym. But to say the truth I have little taste for this sort of work, the style of which in a good deal of current literature is generally cheap and sometimes nasty. It is all very well to write about one's own house, 'Terra-cottage' for example, but to pry into the secrets of other homes, *dulces* or *amaræ* as the case may be, to accept the hospitality of their inmates and then hold them up to ridicule, is at the best but a shabby trick.

I have endeavoured therefore to keep clear of all personal allusions in my book, and if any ingenious friend lights upon a passage which he supposes refers to himself, let me assure him that he is mistaken. These pages may be dull, trivial, commonplace if you please, but at least they shall not be ill-natured.

Social acquaintance in London goes on increasing like a snowball, and unfortunately the larger it becomes the less we can detect in it the flavour of friendship.

I daresay that in provincial towns of which I have seen little or nothing since my boyhood, old cronies, who have known each other from youth up, meet often, interchange greetings of real affection, indulge in local gossip at the dinner table, interchange good stories to which all the guests listen without feeling bored, or hobnobbing, *tête-à-tête* converse in mutual confidence on family affairs, with a full assurance of interest and sympathy on either side. A dim and far-off recollection of my own paternal roof helps me to imagine the possibility of such intercourse, simple, honest, cordial as it might be, and such an ideal of friendship almost compensates for what most cockneys would consider the insufferable dulness of country life.

But in the vast majority of London houses, the present condition of our social system is absolutely inconsistent with sustained intimacy. We don't even know our nearest neighbours, and if we did, on which of them could we drop in casually with the assurance of a welcome? Men, it is true, meet at their clubs, discuss politics, retail town gossip, or prose about business matters, but they know nothing of each other's families, and amidst the whirl and struggle of daily work or pleasure have hardly time to inquire. Even their wives who have an 'at home' day, find few opportunities for private conversation on domestic affairs in a room full of callers, before all of whom it would be embarrassing to speak freely. What *do* women talk about on these occasions? Even in the presence of her lord and master, the British matron is often garrulous. What she must become when left to her own unguided instincts and the society of her own sex, Heaven only knows.

Once, by a rare accident, I returned home early on one of my wife's 'Tuesday afternoons' and found her in the drawing-room surrounded by a throng of visitors. The volume of human voices which reached me down two flights of stairs was quite extraordinary. It suggested a stage chorus—a Sunday-school feast—a vestry meeting. I opened the door and espied a very mild curate, a retired admiral, and an unsuccessful poet—all the rest were ladies—most of them young and voluble. I am rather of a shy disposition, and I confess it was too much for me. Luckily, our page-boy was following close at my heels. With great presence of mind I pushed him in, shut the door and fled to my study. I hope I was unobserved, but since then I have taken care on Tuesdays only to return home just in time for dinner.

During the season, our dining-room mantelpiece is crammed with invitation cards for dinners, after-noon and evening 'at homes,' garden parties, and what not, to which most middle-aged folks are bidden by a liberal, if somewhat tardy fate. Twenty years ago—when one had a keen zest for such entertainments, these invitations came sparingly. Now that one is approaching an age when 'life seems tolerable but for its amusements,' as the late Sir George Cornewall Lewis rather gloomily observed, they are as plentiful as blackberries.

What can weak mortals do? No reasonable man cares to drive out more than three times in a week. As for evening crushes, with a long *queue* of guests swarming up the narrow staircase of a house in Mayfair, or overflowing into the conservatory, while a professional soprano screams in the back drawing-room, or Herr von Strummelkind bangs away at the piano, I frankly admit that they bore me to death. They become a penance even when one has 'come on,' as the phrase is, from a neighbouring dinner. But to dress in cold blood at 10 P.M., and drive, perhaps, a couple of miles to one of these gatherings when the hall barometer registers 70° Fahrenheit, and the average standing room is eighteen inches square, is more than I can dare to venture on.

Some people adopt this form of hospitality on economical grounds, and there is no doubt that it saves a great deal of trouble and expense. Indeed, with a large circle of acquaintances and a moderate income, how is the unfortunate householder to keep pace with his more affluent friends? When the De Cashleighs make two of the dozen guests around my table—we can never sit more than fourteen in our little dining-room—I am haunted by foolish fears and misgivings. I cannot afford to give ninety shillings a dozen for my claret, and I am certain that, at the first sip, the wealthy merchant will detect mine as being of second growth. The Hon. Mrs. De Cashleigh (for he married a peer's daughter) must infallibly notice that our grapes are not the production of an English hot-house, and that the spoons and forks which she handles so daintily with her jewelled fingers do not glitter with that irreproachable brightness which distinguishes her own family plate. Nay, I feel sure that she recognises the features of honest Jenkins, who, though he lived for fifteen years as butler to a Cabinet Minister and now lets lodgings in Half Moon Street, never was in my service—except temporarily, and at the rate of half a guinea per night. I know that it is deplorably weak to bother oneself with such reflections, but they occur nevertheless.

My wife, on the other hand, whom Nature has endowed with more confidence, and perhaps with greater power of observation than myself, assures me that our professed cook (whose assistance may be secured for a modest fee) is quite as accomplished an artist as the De Cashleigh's own *chef*—that they always do justice to our little feasts, and are far more cheerful than in their own house, where it must be confessed they seem to suffer from a depressing sense of propriety.

I suppose it falls to the fate of most average Londoners to find themselves occasionally in certain social circles which differ, to a great extent, from that formed by their own immediate friends. These differences may be generally classed under three heads, viz., those caused by wealth, rank, and intellect, and of these three I fancy the first is really the most formidable. Personally my acquaintance with the 'great world' is limited, partly, no doubt, because I never courted it.

Indolence, shyness, self-respect, to say nothing of other reasons, force upon some men and women the conviction they will find the greatest social happiness in their own set. That that conviction is not shared by us all is proved every day. The special devotion to art, science, or literature which helps a man of genius or untiring industry to make a name in the world is not more remarkable and scarcely less frequent than the ceaseless ambition which prompts certain zealots to run after what is called smart society. It is a form of enthusiasm often rewarded by success, especially among those who watch their chances, give time and trouble to the pursuit, and are not discouraged by occasional rebuffs.

I know a few indefatigable students of the profession whose names are better known in London than if they had been distinguished poets, soldiers, or statesmen. They haunt fashionable re-unions, go to dandy weddings, and get their presence duly chronicled in the 'Morning Post.' They have no more right to this distinction than you or I; yet somehow they achieve it. Through life tbey have lost no opportunity of cultivating the acquaintance of the great. They move heaven and earth to make a few friends in the peerage. Occasionally, of course, they are snubbed, but that does not deter them from further trials. They go on with wonderful perseverance, and in due time their efforts are rewarded.

Your social philosopher smiles at this misdirected and somewhat ignoble energy. To him a man with a handle to his name is neither better nor worse than ordinary mortals. Indeed, when his title is hereditary he may possibly be a very commonplace person after all. In the days of my green youth I used to believe that the perfection of what we call good breeding was always found in association with gentle birth. A man need not reach middle age before he becomes disillusioned on this point. We learn by degrees that both good and bad manners exist in every rank of life.

Some of us have occasionally met with rudeness even in exalted circles. Many of us have recognised the most exquisite sense of courtesy in an Italian peasant.

As a rule it must be admitted that the nobility of this country are simpler in their habits, more gracious in intercourse, and far less ostentatious among their social inferiors than is the case in more than one foreign country which could be named. The same may be said to a great extent respecting our men of real intellect. One of the most modest and kindly hearted gentlemen whom I ever met was a former President of the Royal Society, whose brain was stored with every sort of learning, whose life was one perpetual round of industry, but who in his moments of leisure would talk frankly and affably on comparatively trivial matters. I have known him listen without impatience to the prattle of shallow youngsters and women's artless gossip. One almost forgot the depths of science which he had probed—the physical problems which he had set himself to solve—so genial and cheery was his ordinary bearing.

Your second-rate man of genius, your 'superior person' as he has been aptly styled, is often a very different sort of creature. He will let you know in the course of ten minutes' conversation what a clever fellow he is, and if you only give him time enough will put you right about every subject in creation. If you venture to differ from him, even on a matter to which you may have given special attention, he stops you with a withering smile, as if he really pitied your ignorance. It never occurs to him that there may be two sides to a question. He has spoken, and the rest of the world must take his *dictum* as gospel truth. Society abounds with prigs of this description, and it is a curious fact that though individually they are hated, society comes in time to accept them as authorities on many a matter about which they preach with far more assurance than actual knowledge.

What will not fashion tolerate from those who, practised in the art of *réclame*, and gifted by nature with consummate impudence, have elbowed their way to the front, and by hook or by crook succeeded in getting themselves talked about? Those of my readers who have reached middle age will remember a time when social success under these conditions would have been regarded as phenomenal. It is now a thing of everyday occurrence. Indeed, if a man once succeeds in attaining notoriety—in what line does not much matter—he seems to be welcomed everywhere. He may be consumed by conceit; he may have the manners of a billiard-marker; but provided he has made a *hit*, every one wants to know him.

The tendency of modern London life is, I think, to increase one's acquaintance rather than to promote friendship. Among the endless dinner parties to which many of us are bidden, among the scores of houses where our wives or sisters exchange visits, which is the feast, what is the home where the presence of one guest is valued more than that of any who were there yesterday, or are coming to-morrow? The range of social obligations, of mutual hospitality, has become too wide and comprehensive to admit of much personal intimacy. Our good hostess greets us with a smile and a few casual remarks about the weather or what not, and straightway proceeds to shake hands with Mr. Jones or Lord Robinson, and perhaps to address them in the same terms. The whole entertainment assumes the nature of a function, courteously and liberally performed it is true, but still a function. Only on a few thresholds are we conscious of that genuine and hearty welcome which in less formal life awaits the entry of a friend.

For my own part I would rather see honest Betty's rosy cheeks lighted up with a genial smile as she helps me to take off my coat in the hall of a cottage at Wandsworth, than be received by three solemn footmen at a Belgravian mansion. I don't say that one may not find quite as good friends in an establishment *de luxe* as in humble quarters. All I maintain is that in the bustle and glare of London gaieties, the loyalty of old attachments, the keen sympathy which draws men or women together, find few opportunities for expression.

But being condemned by an inexorable fate to reside in this 'dear, damned, distracting town' (as Pope hath it), we must make the best of it. And looking back on the early days of our housekeeping, the *res angusta domi* period, when the resources of our little *menage* were limited, but when nevertheless we received disinterested kindness and hospitality in many a home long since broken up, I am thankful that the time has arrived when we, in our turn, can welcome to Terra-cottage a large circle of friends, including the sons and daughters of our own former hosts, with many others whom in bygone years I should no more have attempted to entertain than I could have dared to invite Haroun Alraschid, or the Grand Lama of Tibet.

If I refrain from mentioning some of the distinguished guests who have sat at my table, it is out of regard for those readers who, misinterpreting my object, might possibly suspect me of 'side.' Yet I am glad to feel that I have never manœuvred to make acquaintance among people on account of their social rank or worldly means. In the course of my journey through life, I have met not a few of each class. If they care for the society of a man who is neither titled, rich, nor a genius, I am charmed to see them in Dexter Square, but I have never made a favour of their coming. Social ambition may perhaps be followed by material advantages, but if carried too far it is attended by many drawbacks, inconsistent as it seems to me with the repose, simplicity, and happiness which should characterise a quiet English home, even in bustling London.

> Hæc est
> Vita solutorum miserâ ambitione gravique ;
> His me consolor, victurum suavius, ac si
> Quæstor avus, pater atque meus patruusque fuissent.

So Horace argued more than nineteen centuries ago. And what he said then is true unto this day.

CHAPTER XI

OUR NEIGHBOURHOOD

'Terra-cottage,' as I have already explained, is the name facetiously given to our house on account of its colour, and it occupies an unobtrusive position on one side of Dexter Square which lies *dos-à-dos* to Sinister Square—that is to say, each square has a public garden at the back, and the two squares are divided by a street. This description may seem an unnecessary detail to the reader, but I have had to repeat it a score of times to our friends, who cannot be brought to understand why, when they are walking down the street above mentioned, they find the houses of Dexter Square on one side and Sinister Square on the other.

The coachmen of private carriages are equally puzzled. It is of course beneath their dignity to ask the way. They only read the numbers and then the chances are that they stop at the wrong door. Then they cross the road and find that that won't do either, and it generally ends by their driving all round the four sides of each square before they find the right house. As for cabmen, whose feelings are less under control, they indulge in dreadful invectives over the dilemma. 'Blowed if I ever see such a place!' exclaimed a plethoric 'growler' to me one evening. 'Yer never know which square you're in; might as well be in the [*strong adjective*] maze at 'Ampton Court as try and find yer way about 'ere. Why, that's wuth another sixpence!'

Guests are frequently late for dinner in consequence of the same cause, and if two houses bearing the same number provide an entertainment on the same evening the result may be awkward. One night, when we had asked a few friends to dine with us, a man with whom I had a slight acquaintance, but whom I had not invited, was announced at the drawing-room door, bowed to my wife and two or three ladies among our party, and then began to stroll about as if he were looking for some one. At last he came up to me, shook hands, saying in a cheerful tone:

'Very glad to meet *you* here. Quite an unexpected pleasure.' I was nearly reciprocating the compliment but just stopped in time. 'Could my wife have made any mistake?' thought I. 'Had she misdirected a letter, or what?' It was really very embarrassing.

'I hope I am not too early,' he added gaily, pulling out his watch.

'It's not eight o'clock yet,' I stammered out.

'I was invited at 7.45,' he went on, 'but — '

'But what?' I asked innocently.

'Why, the fact is,' he added in a half whisper, 'I don't see our good host in the room.'

'The deuce you don't!' I replied in some surprise; 'why, to whose house do you think you have come?'

'Whose house?' he repeated in amazement, 'why, to Mr. Justice Cramwell's, of course, 87 Sinister Square.

'My dear sir,' said I, 'this house is 87 *Dexter* Square, and it happens to be MINE!'

He uttered a ghastly laugh, pressed my hand by way of apology, and fled precipitately from the room.

. . . .

Although mistakes of this kind are annoying to householders on both sides of the street, a friendly feeling prevails between the two squares. Calls are exchanged between the ladies of each quadrangle, and should conversation flag (which to do their sex justice is of rare occurrence) they amuse themselves by comparing notes as to the relative advantages of their abodes. The Dexter Square drawing-rooms, I hear, are not quite so long as those on the other side of the street. But, on the other hand, our bedrooms are more commodious. The Sinister side residents have a bigger conservatory than we can boast, but their areas are not so spacious as ours, and so forth.

When we dine with each other—unless it is pelting with rain—we dispense with cabs. Our womankind shroud themselves in cloaks and wrappers and we are over the way in half a minute. There is a generous rivalry in the management of the two square gardens. I always maintain that ours looks the smartest, but then as a Dexterite I am bound to think so. Once we formed a joint committee for the purpose of putting down street nuisances—barrel-organs, and the yells of Sunday newsboys, &c. The meetings were conducted with the utmost propriety, and we read a pile of correspondence on the subject. But as half the inhabitants on both sides seemed to derive great pleasure from listening to a hurdy-gurdy, and the other half thought that if we attempted to stop the sale of kitchen newspapers it would be interfering with the rights of THE PEOPLE, we abandoned our measures of reform as a bad job, and the interests of music and literature remain unaffected.

The police authorities evidently regard us as a law-abiding community, not requiring much supervision. It is the rarest thing in the world to find a constable in the neighbourhood. I searched for one once during the great part of an hour while seven 'froze out' gardeners, who looked like convicts out for a spree, rent the air with a mighty roar. But when I appealed to X 99 he demurred, asked me whether I was prepared to give the men in charge, and walked at a deliberate pace to the scene of disturbance about a quarter of a mile off. When we reached it, of course, the vocalists had disappeared.

As to Sunday newsboys I have waged war on my own account, but, I regret to add, ineffectually. They begin about 8 A.M. and go on almost incessantly until half-past one. I have watched them and listened to them so often and so long that I could give some curious statistics on the subject of their calling, or, to speak more accurately, their *screeching*. They vary in age, in size, in impudence, and in attire, but they possess one faculty in common which I have never known to fail--I mean strength of lung. Some of their voices are as shrill as the noise made by an un-greased cart-wheel; others attain the accents of an angry bull. But I never saw one yet who did not succeed in making himself heard from the north-west corner of one square to the south-east corner of the other. The average number of cries which they utter in one minute is at least ten. There are sixty minutes in an hour, and as the performance usually extends over five hours, you arrive by a simple process of arithmetic at 3,000 cries on every blessed Sabbath morning. It is true that by going to church one may avoid 1,200 of them, but I put it to any orthodox Christian whether the balance of 1,800 is a fitting prelude to one's devotions. Besides, if it is necessary for me to go to church, it is equally necessary for the newsboy. If a special mission should ever be organised for the purpose of securing their attendance at morning service, I will subscribe my guinea cheerfully.

Of course all the papers sold are for kitchen reading. What is the peculiar charm about 'Boyd's Weekly Noose' and journals of that class which attracts our cooks and housemaids? I have told my servants over and over again that they are welcome to read all the broad sheets—morning, evening, and special editions which we take in ourselves. I don't interfere with their politics. They might have the 'Britannia,' the 'Planet,' the 'Reverberator,' the 'Back-stairs' (a penny Society paper), or any other entertaining publication which they prefer, provided that it is delivered on Saturday night. But it won't do. There must be some fascination about that Sunday yell. They like to run up the area steps, waylay the ragged little urchin on his rounds, and take their pennyworth of rubbish fresh from his hands.

On week-days the itinerant chair-mender perambulates Dexter Square and its neighbourhood at a funereal pace, uttering incessantly about the most dismal wail that ever issued from a human throat.

It is impossible to give in printers' ink any adequate notion of that weird and dreary cry. Reproach, anguish, and despair are all embodied in its accents. It begins with a bellow and ends with a whine. The last notes, pitched in a minor key, have scarcely died away before the cry begins again. Why the business of chair-mending should be proclaimed in such lugubrious tones passes my comprehension. Personally I should have regarded it as rather a cheerful pursuit, involving no responsibility, a very small outlay of capital, and not much manual labour. But, however that may be, a still more wonderful problem remains to be solved. What householders employ these wandering craftsmen?

I have lived in Dexter Square for nearly twenty years, and up to the present time I have never seen a single chair handed out to mend. The work can always be done, and cheaply enough, in the shops. Where do the peripatetic chair-menders get a job? I have sometimes been uncharitable enough to imagine that the whole thing is a sham, that they are area-sneaks in disguise, or are in collusion with professional burglars. It is certain that most of them are gipsies, who we know have the credit of never losing an opportunity. I tackled one of them some years ago and asked him who were his customers. He answered, sharply enough, that that was his business. Apologising for my inquisitiveness, I reminded him that I saw him every morning looking out for work, but that he never seemed to get any.

'Ah,' he said, 'I dessay you get all your work done for you. Somebody else made all your money I'll be bound. You've only got to spend it.'

I told him he was mistaken on that point, and that I had to work for my living like many others.

'Well I does the same,' growled the gipsy. 'Wot then?'

I told him that I had not the slightest objection to his form of industry, if he did not make such a noise over it.

'Wot's the odds?' he said. 'Wot 'arm comes of it?'

'Well,' I answered, 'perhaps it interferes with other people's work. It certainly does with mine.'

He looked at me for a moment in silence, but with an expression of supreme contempt.

'Crikey!' he said at last; 'well that is a rum 'un. Can't abear to 'ear me a hollerin, can't yer? *Why, yer see, you are one o' them chaps as ought to live in Epping Forest!*'

. . . . . .

This retort absolutely quenched me, and I have never attempted to question a chair-mender since.

. . . . . .

There is a story about a stupid old lady, who once remarked how providential it was that most capital towns and great cities have a big river flowing through them. With equal truth I might observe that our residential neighbourhood is lucky in its proximity to that thoroughfare of shops—Eastbourne Avenue. There is something about its very name which savours of sylvan simplicity. Perhaps, once upon a time, it really was a grove, planted with elms or poplars, which have long since been cut down for firewood and 'vanished into thin air.

Anyhow, there is something about the street which is unlike most London streets devoted to business. A sort of *rus-in-urbe* character still clings to it. It is like a street in some lazy country town or idle watering-place. Foot passengers don't hurry through it, but walk along, leisurely stopping now and then to chat with each other, or look into the shop windows. The florists, the greengrocers, the confectioners, even the bootmakers and haberdashers who occupy both sides of the road, seem to be easy-going people, who greet you with a smile when you enter their establishments, and don't look you up and down as they do in Oxford Street or Regent Street. The young men inside wait patiently while you select what you want, and don't drum their fingers on the counter with impatience, as I have noticed they sometimes do elsewhere. The managers will cheerfully send home goods on what they call *appro'*. If you live in Dexter Square and present your card, they nod with deference and say it is all right. You belong to the neighbourhood and the neighbourhood is respectable. There is a sort of *esprit de corps* about the locality, which is pleasant.

There are several big shops in the street, but the biggest of all is Blackwood's. It occupies about a third of the best part of Eastbourne Avenue, and has an enormous frontage in the road round the corner. Every year some addition is made to the premises, and if things go on at this rate, the business of the whole thoroughfare will be absorbed in a monopoly.

Blackwood calls himself the COSMOPOLITAN CATERER, and he really deserves the title. There is scarcely a branch of human industry unrepresented in his gigantic emporium. Tailoring, dressmaking, millinery, hats, boots and gloves; cabinet-work, carpets, curtains and crockery; bed linen and kitchen utensils; portmanteaus and garden tools; picture frames and stationery; wines and provisions of every sort and kind; luncheon-rooms, hair-dressing and reading-rooms. Agencies without end, for engaging a servant up to buying a house. I don't know whether there is a matrimonial department there yet, but I am always expecting that Blackwood will extend his business in that direction. There might be a difficulty about sending out wives *on appro'*, but one may be sure that a man of Blackwood's genius would surmount it. It is said that a facetious customer, in order to test the great CATERER's ingenuity, once asked him if he could procure an elephant. The wretched trifler was at once referred to the zoological department, where he found an official ready to book the order.

I am afraid to say how many 'hands' are employed at Blackwood's. Many hundreds certainly—and for what I know the number may reach thousands. To watch them all trooping out into the 'Avenue' after shop hours is a truly wonderful sight. There is such a crowd that for a while passenger traffic is impeded. Most of the *employés* are lodged and boarded, I am told, at the great caterer's expense. The young men are accommodated in one set of buildings and the young women in others. Comfort and cleanliness prevail throughout, and the daily fare is said to be excellent. What a family to provide for! What a community to supervise! What an establishment to maintain! Here is a huge concourse of human beings to be housed, fed, washed, recreated, marshalled and disciplined daily.

And all this quasi-parental care is but an incident in the vast system of organisation required for the management of a gigantic business. Why, the master of a big public school, the head of a great bank, enjoys a sinecure compared with such responsibility. The man who can undertake the duties of such a position and discharge them successfully is fit to command an army or be a colonial governor.

Rumours have been rife concerning Blackwood's official relations to the great commercial house associated with his name. It has been alleged that it really belongs to a company of which he is but the manager. A wealthy nobleman's name has been mentioned in connection with the enterprise. Some say that the whole concern is financed by a well-known firm of millionaires. If so, the secret has been well kept, for nothing is definitely known except that, to all appearance, Blackwood is the acknowledged chief—'BOSS' I think the Americans call it—of the colossal institution in Eastbourne Avenue. His authority there is supreme. You may see the great man himself walking quietly about from department to department with a calm air of self-possession and easy confidence, as though shop-keeping on this extraordinary scale was quite a pleasant pastime, and to be a COSMOPOLITAN CATERER involved no more anxiety than might be felt by a master of the ceremonies.

His admirers love to say that he began life with half-a-crown, but that has been asserted of so many successful men that the tradition has become stale and wearisome. It is certain that he rose from the humble position of a small tradesman in the Avenue to be the head of an establishment which is known all over London—over England—and, in a commercial sense, over half of civilised Europe.

Blackwood, like all great men, has had to endure the penalties of success. Owners of adjacent shops smile satirically when his name is mentioned. I am not surprised. They would be more than human if they watched with complacency the progress of a huge rival business which threatens to absorb their own. Smart society, too, sneers at Blackwood's. Yet, somehow, his shop is often thronged with ladies of fashion, and in the season you will be sure to find a dozen or more of well-appointed carriages waiting for his customers in the Avenue. For my own part—like most men, I hate shopping, but to women who take an unaffected pleasure in the pastime it must be convenient to buy all they want under one roof. You can spend hours if you like in the place, passing from department to department until your purse and your patience are exhausted, and then take lunch or afternoon tea.

There are cashiers all over the place, for you must pay money down or settle the account on delivery. The bills—for they have been shown to me sometimes—fill me with awe and amazement. They contain a greater number of farthings than I have ever seen since I first learnt compound arithmetic. Every item seems to be charged for in fractions of copper coin. It would drive me distracted to add them up. Yet our wives and daughters solve the problem cheerfully. To those mysterious farthings, and the NO CREDIT system —to small profits and quick returns, backed by a capacity for organisation—Blackwood owes his success.

I don't know that our neighbourhood can boast of being a particularly religious one, but, if it fails in its morals, no one can say that our spiritual requirements are neglected. We are a mixed community, but nearly every creed is represented by a substantial edifice. Within a few minutes' walk from Dexter Square there are at least a half-dozen churches of the Establishment where the service, doctrine, and sermon are such as to satisfy every shade of Anglican faith. A Roman Catholic fraternity have their college and chapel in an adjacent street. Conventicles and meeting-houses abound in the minor thoroughfares. The Greeks have a large and imposing temple of their own, and almost within sight of its porch there is a handsome synagogue.

It is pleasant to watch the respective congregations trooping towards these buildings once a week, and to remember—notwithstanding all our romantic regrets as to the past—that the *odium theologicum* which raged a few centuries ago is becoming gradually obliterated; and that, meanwhile, people are far better taught, the poor far more largely helped, the sick far more cared for, and dumb animals far more protected than was the case in the much vaunted ages of faith when orthodoxy prevailed, and covered a multitude of sins: when religion lacked charity, tolerated selfishness, winked at vice, and sometimes led to crime.

In those days some of our neighbours, differing from each other perhaps respecting the shortest road to Heaven, would have been divided on this fair earth by a greater gulf than Dives and Lazarus in Hades. Friendship would have been impossible between Jew and Christian, Churchman and Dissenter, Romanist and Schismatic. In civilised England—except among a few fanatics—sectarian animosities are now well-nigh ignored. And so these good people, flocking east or west towards their several houses of prayer, forget for a moment their spiritual divergencies, and exchange a pleasant smile or friendly greeting as they pass.

Some day hence, may be, what you believe and I believe will not appear so vastly inconsistent. Each of us may have been somewhat mistaken in our convictions, or we may have expressed them inaccurately. And if we don't find this out during our earthly lot, let us hope that it may be revealed to us by-and-by in another and better NEIGHBOURHOOD.

Our house, as I have already said, is within a short distance from Kensington Gardens, so that in three minutes' walk we can reach that delightful retreat, the quietest, the most pleasant and picturesque that I know in any capital of Europe. To live close to this little sylvan paradise, lying in the midst of noisy, smoky London, is a blessed privilege which I would not forego, no, not for the sake of a house twice as big as ours, and in a far smarter neighbourhood. The very proximity of such a large open space, with its wide expanse of green turf, its venerable trees (a large number of which still remain, notwithstanding the ruthless thinning which took place some years ago); its ornamental waters, its shady walks, its cheery flower beds and its stately old palace, is a source of joy.

Early in the morning, when few people are about and the air is fresh, when you lose sight of Kensington Gore and the Bayswater road, and get away from the noise and turmoil of the streets, you may almost forget London and imagine yourself in the country. To sit, in early summertime, under the shade of a fine chestnut tree laden with blossom and before its young leaves have become soiled by smoke—to hear the notes of a real thrush or blackbird in its branches, to look down the long vista of an avenue and see the bright green foliage set against a hazy distance of deep violet, is, for cockney human nature, an inestimable boon.

Even the sheep browsing here and there give a pastoral appearance to the scene, especially the new-comers, before their wool has had time to get dusky.

A landscape painter might find a dozen charming subjects in these fair Gardens, if he had but the courage to set up his easel there, but you rarely see one. Sometimes, indeed, a lady amateur will take her sketch book and try to convey an impression (in water-colours) of the Palace, the round pond, and the spire of Kensington Church rising into an azure sky, on a sheet of paper measuring about nine inches by six.

But she works, I confess, under difficulties which I should find deterrent. Under the mysterious law which rules town life, she has no sooner planted her camp-stool on the turf and taken up a pencil, than she is surrounded by a crowd of youthful connoisseurs who admire and whisper around her. Children will leave their nursemaids to run up and see what she is doing. The ragged little urchin who has been fishing for stickleback with an old cart-whip and a glass bottle, readily abandons his favourite sport to look at the *lidy droring*. And so the colours are mixed up hastily and splashed on peevishly by our fair student, and in time she loses her patience and spoils her drawing; the sketch-book is at last shut up and the camp-stool folded, and, another work of art is lost to the world.

No, on second thoughts, I cannot recommend

Kensington Gardens as a convenient sketching ground, but it is a delightful lounge and promenade. On week days you may walk about there for hours without meeting more than a dozen people, or you may sit in some secluded spot with a favourite book and read there to your heart's content, undisturbed except by that ubiquitous official who claims a penny for your chair, and then vanishes into obscurity.

Thanks to a merciful fate, perambulators are scarce. I fancy the servant girls who wheel them prefer Hyde Park as being more lively. They can see the carriages there and occasionally meet a Life Guardsman. It is a curious fact about flirtations in their condition of life, that far from assuming a clandestine nature they are usually carried on in the most frank and open manner and in the most conspicuous places. A bench by the side of a public pathway is frequently selected as a suitable spot for the exchange of caresses between Tommy Atkins and his ancillary *chère amie*. Whether it is that they are too much absorbed in mutual admiration to heed the notice of passers by, or whether they rather take a pride in being observed, I cannot say. But certain it is that they do not attempt to make a mystery of their affection. It is all fair and above board, and their courtship is rarely marred by any false delicacy or morbid diffidence.

Higher up in the social scale, people are more

squeamish about these matters, and to them, no doubt, Kensington Gardens seem more suitable for *al fresco* declarations. Strolling all unconsciously under the trees at noontide you may come quite unawares upon some fair damsel who, as she hears your footsteps, raises her eyes suddenly from her novel with an anxious glance around, and then—quite as hastily—seems absorbed in her book again. You walk on demurely with a feeling of half regret that you have inadvertently disturbed her.

A hundred paces or so further on, you meet, perchance, a good-looking man hurrying towards the spot which you have just left. You feel instinctively that it is to keep an appointment. Half a minute later you turn round, of course accidentally, to look at the view, and though the tree trunks half conceal the couple from your sight, you know that they have met. Who is he? Where does he hail from? How can he spare time for this sort of thing—in the middle of the day too? What is she? Why does she meet him here, instead of at her home? How long has she been waiting? When did they arrange this rendezvous? Why do they look cautiously around? (so unlike Tommy Atkins and his sweetheart). You are not naturally inquisitive, but somehow you would like to have some information on these points, if only to clear up your doubts.

Well, well, perhaps it is better that you are not in a position to inquire too closely. There may be a little romance, or there may not. Anyhow, it is no business of yours. Pass on to the open sward, walk round the great pond and look at the old Palace. What a host of memories, historical, political, and social, the building conjures up! You might in imagination fill that fair garden on the south front with a crowd of defunct celebrities, crowned heads, statesmen, courtiers and *grandes dames* who were once associated with the place, but who have since joined the great majority.

What was the original mansion like when it belonged to the Coppins, to the Finches, ages ago, before King William III. bought the house from the Earl of Nottingham and converted it into a royal palace? The Dutch-bred monarch's monogram and that of his English wife may still be seen on some of the portals. Queen Mary, one may be sure, loved the place for the sake of her husband who enlarged and beautified it. It was her sister, Queen Anne, who employed Sir Christopher Wren to design that stately orange house, the finest specimen of brickwork, perhaps, in England. George II. lived here, and Queen Caroline, they say, added largely to the grounds in which Hervey, Chesterfield, and Walpole walked.

Do you remember young Warrington's visit to the

Palace, as described by Thackeray in the 'Virginians'? The old state apartments have long since been dismantled. They fell into disuse after 1760, but illustrious inmates have lingered for generations past in the building. It was here on a bright summer morning in 1837 that Lord Melbourne and the Archbishop of Canterbury brought to the youthful Princess Victoria the news that she was Queen of England, and only last year a marble statue representing that august lady, still young and beautiful, was placed in front of the Palace, where you may see it, modelled by the hands of her accomplished daughter.

CHAPTER XII

'PER STRATA VIARUM'

ALTHOUGH, as I have shown in a previous chapter, our neighbourhood is not entirely free from noises, Terra-cottage seems a perfect haven of rest on returning home after a walk through the great bustling thoroughfares in the busiest part of the West End. I have lived in London, man and boy, for a great many years. I used to love its streets at one time, and to this day I derive a sort of childish pleasure from looking into shop windows.

I like to saunter up Regent Street and along Oxford Street during the season, watching the carriages, landaus, broughams, and what not, drawn by well-bred, high mettled horses, with a couple of sprucely liveried servants on each box. I enjoy the sight of these equipages, I say, often filled with some of the loveliest and most refined women in the world, who daintily trip across the pavement to interview their milliners, add to their stock of jewellery, or choose a new carpet for the drawing-room. It is pleasant to meet an honest, healthy looking country squire beguiled by his blooming wife and pretty daughters into a little pedestrian shopping.

I notice cheery looking country cousins, young subalterns in mufti, and dandy undergraduates piloting their fair sisters along the crowded *trottoir*. A troop of Horse Guards on their chargers ambling along the thoroughfare to their barracks, clad in magnificent uniform, with their sabres and cuirasses gleaming in the sunshine; a display of Oriental china and choice bric-à-brac in Liberty's warehouse; a group of flower girls seated at the base of some public monument making up their nosegays, even a file of sandwich men (so long as they keep clear of the pavement) grotesquely costumed in the interest of some new advertisement. All these and countless other objects in London street life are, I submit, legitimate attractions to any man with a sense of the picturesque who can afford time to walk as he goes forth daily to his labour until the evening.

But every pleasure has its drawback, and, alas! that of lingering in the streets, even the best and gayest streets, of London is fast becoming obsolete. In the first place, they are too crowded. The good, old-fashioned rule—the *lex inscripta* once universally recognised by cockney pedestrians of keeping on the right hand of the gangway is no longer observed. Stragglers dodge from one side of the pavement to the other, and when you meet them (the women are always the worst in this respect) they carefully move to right or left in the *same* direction as yourself, which to a well ordered mind is an awful aggravation. Then there are the perambulators, which for some inscrutable reason are always being dragged diagonally across your path.

The underground electric wires present another form of nuisance, for they are everlastingly being pulled up, and this operation, which even from a scientific point of view would hardly seem to include a single feature of human interest, presents extraordinary attractions to street-cads and loafers who crowd around and watch the workmen with intense curiosity for an hour or two every day.

The peril of street crossings has been somewhat mitigated by the activity of the police, but although they do their best to prevent your being knocked down by omnibuses and carrier-vans, even their official zeal is powerless against the stout old beldame, holding a child in each hand and a formidable umbrella under her arm, who charges down upon you from the other side of the way, while a motley crowd, flanked by match-sellers, penny toy-men, and newsboys collides in all directions between the gutter and the 'refuge.'

Oh! those newsboys! I counted seventeen of them the other evening on one side alone of Piccadilly

Circus. One would think that this number would have sufficed for the supply of journals within the radius of at least a quarter of a mile. But you have scarcely walked a dozen yards up Regent Street before you meet another young ruffian who, not content with making an apron of his 'poster,' bawls out his wares with a deafening yell: 'EVENIN' NOOSE! SPAYSHAWL!! STOR! GLOBOREKKO! SPAYSHAWL! AW THE WEANERS! SPAYSHAWL!!!' and so on. He is scarcely out of sight—and far from out of hearing—when you are overtaken by another demon in human form who renews the shout with increased vigour, until your tortured nerves impel you to turn down the nearest by-street. And, if you do, ten to one but you will encounter a fourth tormentor waiting for you round the corner.

Ah! we are a tolerant and a long-suffering public in this country. Excepting Madrid, which towards evening is, I think, the noisiest capital in Europe, there are few cities where this pestilential nuisance has grown to such magnitude as in London. Of course, if the police or the County Council thought fit, it might be stopped to-morrow. Little *kiosques* might be planted at intervals along every leading thoroughfare where journals of every kind and price—every shade of politics and every tint of paper—might be sold, speedily, peacefully, and profitably, while the cost to ratepayers would hardly exceed a halfpenny in the pound.

But be sure if this plan were adopted, and the hardworking bread-winner were enabled to walk home after his long day's work without being maddened by unnecessary street cries, some idiot would get up in the House of Commons, prate about the rights of the people, and pretend that we had interfered with an honest industry.

As to the recklessness and brutality of street-driving in London, until a bishop or a duke is knocked over, I despair of any attempt to remedy this too fruitful source of accidents. I have seen hansom-cab drivers pale with rage, or perhaps inflamed by drink, flog their horses so unmercifully that if the poor animal had bolted into the nearest shop, kicked the vehicle to pieces, and pitched the cabman head foremost on to the pavement, it would not have been surprising. Indeed, I am not at all sure that a broken leg or arm would be too heavy a penalty for any man who could bring himself to inflict such torture on a horse.

The furious rate at which cabs are often driven through crowded thoroughfares involves a frightful risk to foot passengers. Every day some accident happens, but how often do you hear of cabmen being sent to gaol for assault or homicide? In nine cases out of ten they get off with a fine, or a temporary suspension of license. I have been a London householder for more than a quarter of a century, and I have never yet seen a policeman attempt to stop a cab driven at dangerous speed, or try to take its number. In such cases, indeed, the 'force' on foot is no force at all. Mounted constables are just as much needed in the streets as in the parks—and we shall get them—some time in the Greek Kalends.

The bicycle plague is a novel one—novel at least to middle-aged Englishmen. There has been a great deal of grumbling about it in the newspapers, but so far as London is concerned, nothing has yet been done to stop it. A year or two ago some worthy magistrate delivered an authoritative opinion on the bench that bicycles were subject to the same rules as other wheeled vehicles, that is to say, that they must not be ridden at a speed which would be considered dangerous in a carriage. Bless the honest Beak's heart! Why, scarcely a day passes without one's seeing bicycles ridden at the rate of ten, fifteen, almost twenty miles an hour by semi-circular idiots who, in the twinkling of an eye, outstrip every cab and omnibus on the road, cutting diagonally across the course of private carriages, frightening the horses, provoking coachmen to frightful invective, impeding foot traffic, alarming women and children, terrifying the infirm, and only escaping actual homicide by a hair's breadth. And then these lunatics excuse themselves by saying that if a collision were to take place, they (the riders) would be likely to suffer most! But this is an argument which so far as I can see might with equal justice be urged by a dynamitard who carries about an explosive in his pocket. Neither murder nor manslaughter can be palliated by such a plea. The reckless bicyclist ought to be suppressed as soon as possible. Philanthropy should put a spoke in his wheel!

As for light and jaunty parcel vans, juggernautish carrier waggons, and butchers' carts out on practice for a sharp trotting match against time, I would levy a substantial deodand on their owners and send their drivers to prison with hard labour for six months after every accident for which they were found responsible. If Britannia, who has been ruling the waves for so many generations past, were to spare a little time for the regulation of street traffic those of her sons who reside in London would have much reason to be grateful.

Omnibuses, too, and omnibus ways are woefully in need of reform. They are too numerous; they are too cumbersome; they carry too many passengers; they are cruelly heavy for the horses; they jostle and race with each other to the risk of life; they are obstacles to progress in the road of civilisation. Under proper management they might become a blessing to the public; as it is, they are in many ways an insufferable nuisance.

To begin with, I suppose there is no city in the world where the conductor of a public vehicle would be permitted to make such an unnecessary noise over his work as a London 'bus-cad. Omnibuses ply daily through the streets of Paris, Berlin, Vienna, Munich, Milan, Florence, and a dozen other large towns, but they are driven and attended by rational beings, who do not make day and night hideous by shouting out an utterly unintelligible jargon, incessantly repeated with 'damnable iteration' without serving in the slightest degree a reasonable purpose. I suppose I shall be told that it is for the information of the public. But what public? Every Londoner who hails a 'bus knows by its colour what line of route it will follow, and if there is any doubt on that point, the name inscribed in huge capitals on the side will inform him. More than this, every street or station of importance near which the omnibus passes is legibly printed in bold letters, and, thanks to the School Board, even the humblest passenger can read nowadays.

But then, it will be said, we are not all Londoners. Some of us may be country cousins unfamiliar with the ways of town and the titles of districts. Well, supposing you are a mere rustic, from Dartmoor, let us say, or Lincolnshire, or the Isle of Skye. You want to know where the 'bus is going and you listen for the conductor's information. Will anyone outside the walls of Hanwell pretend that he is enlightened by such ejaculations as 'CHIPCYDERBAG! LOOPHOLE STREET RAIRWAY! OBUN-ERSTEE!!' An old cockney going into the City might by long experience translate this gibberish to himself, but to your ordinary yeoman it would be simply unintelligible.

When I first came to London it took me a long time to discover that 'RYE-LOOK' meant a well known tavern in Bayswater, that ''GENT'S CUSS,' 'TORIERTEVEN,' 'LAND-PORK,' and ''PERDS BO!' all indicated a westward route. To this day in an unfamiliar district I confess I am puzzled. But, nevertheless, the yells go on at the rate of ten in a minute. I know a conductor who bawls out 'MOBBY LARCH!' on an average seventy times between Oxford Circus and Hyde Park. He might just as well—so far as any practical good is concerned, cry 'NEBUCHADNEZZAR' or 'PARALLELOGRAM!' No one understands what he says, except those who don't want to be informed—and everyone is tortured by the ceaseless shouting which never has added twopence to the conductor's takings, and never will.

The ways of London omnibuses are mysterious and wonderful. They linger unnecessarily long at certain stations, causing immense inconvenience to street traffic. It is only under pressure that they can be got to start at all. Yet once on the road the 'bus-cad considers it almost a personal favour to let you put your foot on the step before he sends on the horses at full gallop and you are hurled staggering to your seat. Women are often dragged into the vehicle with no more care than if they were so many bales of jute. Remonstrance is useless; 'WOT ARE YOU TALKING ABOUT? MUST KEEP OUR TIME, MUSTN'T WE?' exclaims the conductor with lofty indignation, and yet, perhaps, he has been dawdling for ten minutes at the 'MOBBY LARCH!'

It is, perhaps, a misplaced respect for this plea which induces nimble young counter-jumpers to drop out of the 'bus while it is in full speed. One of these days a dislocated ankle may cure them of the practice, but I believe that nothing, not even the loss of a fellow passenger's eye, will reform the idiot who enters an omnibus carrying his stick or umbrella like a spear.

And this reminds me of another fatuous and wholly inexplicable custom which, apparently originating at Earlswood, has gradually spread over London: I mean the monstrous fashion of carrying sticks and umbrellas with their handles downwards. I have shared many follies with the companions of my early youth, but this is a kind of imbecility which transcends anything that I can remember. Personally, I would as soon think of wearing my coat inside out, or putting my left glove on my right hand, as of carrying my umbrella upside down. But nineteen out of twenty 'mashers' do so. Indeed, I have seen grey-haired old fogeys, who ought to know better, infected by this form of mania. The worst of it is that they seem to recover their senses when they enter an omnibus and at once proceed to *reverse arms*, a process which, as the lumbering vehicle jogs onwards, adds certain danger to supreme folly.

But this does not exhaust the amenities of omnibus travelling in London. There is the inevitable old lady who knows as well as you or I that there is a rail inside near the roof by which she can hold as she passes to her seat, but who, nevertheless, thinks that it is consistent with advanced civilisation in a Christian country to clutch at her fellow passengers' knees and shoulders, and use them as props until she has found her place. There is the City man of sixteen stone with a capacious waistcoat, who makes a point of sitting with his legs very wide apart and occupying twice as much space as he has paid for. There is the milliner's girl, who carries on her lap a bandbox big enough to hold a set of gardening tools and who eats an apple with great relish *en route*. There is, thanks to the penny fares, the laundress with her bundle, who brings a fine odour of peppermint [I hope it is only peppermint] into the carriage; and finally there is our old friend the conductor again, who whistles a music-hall air while he issues his tickets, stamps on the floor of the 'bus or blows through a bird-call in preference to ringing the bell when he wants the driver to stop.

Ah! 'they manage these things better in France,' or, for that matter, in Germany too, but then we are freeborn Britons and will put up with anything.

Among the various scenes illustrative of town life, which supplied the pencil of John Leech with subjects for ridicule, there are few to which he devoted himself more heartily than those in which cabmen and their 'fares' used to figure as the *dramatis personæ*. With what wondrous skill and truthfulness that ingenious caricaturist brought before us a red-nosed, many-caped charioteer doubling or trebling his legitimate charge, or the satirical Jehu returning the proffered shilling with a scornful suggestion that his employer might require it for a washing bill; or the Hansom offering to drive a nervous gentleman 'out of his mind, for eighteenpence.' The wretched knock-kneed screw of a horse, the damp and dingy vehicle to which it was harnessed, the ready chaff and impudence of Bardolph on the box-seat, the timid expostulations of passengers, the calm philosophy of the waterman, the *badinage* exchanged with costermongers or the driver of a passing 'bus; all these have formed an endless fund of amusement in our 'London Charivari.'

But, unfortunately, there are many aspects of social life which, though vastly entertaining in the pages of 'Punch,' are by no means pleasant in the light of actual experience. A broken-down cab and a jaded hack, for instance, form exceedingly picturesque materials for a humorous sketch; but in a ride from Belgravia to London Bridge they are not likely to improve one's spirits. We laugh at the driver's insolence when it appears as the legend of a wood-cut; but when we hear it addressed to ourselves *vivâ voce*, we feel inclined to take his number.

Indeed, the discomfort and annoyance to which the cab-hiring public is subject are generally calculated to provoke more indignation than merriment. There is no joke in the fact that the capital city of the richest country in the world is worse provided with public conveyances than a provincial German town. It is no joke first to be cheated and then insulted by an ill-conditioned ruffian who, by coarse vituperation, may succeed in extorting any amount of overcharge, especially if he has ladies to deal with. For when a London cabman is angry he grows abusive, and when he has become abusive, his language is distinguished by powerful adjectives and past participles which are very unpleasant to hear.

It is true that you may compel him to drive you at once to the nearest police-station in case of a dispute. But what proportion of 'fares' have time or inclination to avail themselves of this remedy? A man is hurrying to catch an express train for some distant part of England, or he arrives punctually at a house where he has been invited to dine, or he is set down in some busy thoroughfare in the city, where he has an appointment. Is it likely that any of these would brook the vexatious delay involved by Mr. Fitzroy's Act? Is it probable that a stock-broker, to whom every minute may be of value on 'Change, or a lady who may have already knocked at a friend's door, will sacrifice the best part of an hour in driving to and from a police-station, and there await the decision of Mr. Inspector, all for the sake of a shilling?

No, Mr. Fitzroy! we want better cabs, better cabmen, and better supervision of both. If sixpence a mile is too little to pay the cab proprietor a fair interest on his outlay (and I should like to know what he considers a fair interest), make it eightpence if you like, but let us have respectable drivers and decent cabs, not such a ramshackle concern as one that I heard of the other day, which breaking into two halves on the road, ejected the unfortunate lady who was inside, and left her scarred for life.

And now I must make room for another grumble —about street crossings. Shall we ever live to see the day, I wonder, when they will be swept by order of the County Council? I am a ratepayer, and I would willingly submit to a tax of a penny a day—or, say, 2*l.* a year for the convenience. But I strongly object to give a penny to every crossing-sweep who stands begging for a 'copper' at the corner of every by-street in my daily walk. In the first place, he ought to know by this time that no copper coins are in circulation now; and he ought further to remember that if, during my peregrinations, I were to give him and his brethren a penny apiece, it would cost me at least five shillings a day or nearly 100*l.* per annum. I really can't afford it.

And why am I to make invidious selections? One crossing-sweep in my eyes is as good (or as bad) as another, and the worst of it is that the fee is demanded whether the crossing is dirty or not. I know an ill-favoured old woman who intercepts a congregation on the way to church—no matter what the weather may be. On a dry and frosty morning, when there is not a pinch of dust on the road, there she stands, broom in hand, doing literally nothing for her wage but dropping abject curtseys. But she makes a living out of it, nevertheless!

And now a few more words on the subject of street

mendicancy. I am naturally a soft-hearted creature, and to this day, in spite of experience, I don't like to pass a tramp with his wife and children dragging after him without giving him a trifle. But it is generally admitted that the beggars of London represent a class of vagabonds more numerous in proportion and more distinguished by fraud than exists in any other Western capital.

If we may believe the police, everyone who asks for money in our public thoroughfares is an impostor. Most of them, by keeping within the letter of the law, i.e. by offering a box of matches for sale or carrying a basket of groundsel, can avoid being 'run in,' but they are, as a rule, impostors—and successful ones, too. The best proof of this lies in the fact that hundreds of beggars in this metropolis, however forlorn and wretched their appearance may be, continue, year after year, to ply the same trade under precisely the same conditions as before. Occasionally, it is true, some of them disappear for awhile from the scene of their inactive labours, but that is only to enjoy a brief interval of rest and dissipation, and, this over, each returns to his or her particular beat in the full confidence of an abundant harvest.

Most of this class are so well known to Londoners that it is difficult to conceive why this perpetuated and evidently successful plea of indigence does not in itself awaken suspicion. But there are easy-going philanthropists who would seem either to be indifferent on this point, or actually to recognise a sort of claim in the vagrancy which they encounter under the same stereotyped form every day of their lives. I could mention a dozen examples of street beggars at the West End of town, who, without asking for a single penny, have for years past drained the pockets of the public.

I remember one man who, feigning idiotcy, used to walk along Oxford Street with a kind of tripping gait, his head bent low on his breast, his eyes half closed, and his arms stretched out before him, covered with dingy stay-laces, which, of course, he never sold, but which, being a saleable commodity, sufficed to redeem him from the charge of mendicancy. Another was a robust and sturdy blind beggar, usually dressed in a smockfrock, who, preceded by a little dog which he held by a string, emphatically tapped the pavement before him with a stick and thus called attention to his infirmity. He took care to wear no shade over his sightless eyes, and the deplorable spectacle thus presented at once excited compassion and secured to him a daily source of profit far beyond what he could have hoped to have earned as an able-bodied labourer.

A favourite dodge among blind beggars is to wait at a crossing until someone leads them over, and of course leaves a coin in their hands. Not long ago I watched one of them waiting for this chance, when a crossing-sweep came up and tendered his assistance. I saw the blind man hesitate for a moment, and then *decline* the aid. He probably recognised the boy's voice and knew that he would get nothing out of him. At all events, he turned back and walked in the opposite direction.

Then there is the disconsolate mother, who, with judiciously blanched cheeks and scanty clothing, sits rocking her child—the child that never grows older—in the dark corner of some doorstep. Ever and anon she raises an appealing glance to passers by. One by one the coins drop into her lap and are hastily stowed away beneath her threadbare shawl. If you make inquiry of her she will tell you that she needs medicine for her child, food for herself, a night's lodging, or what not. Yet, strange to say, when ample provision has been made for these wants, she still sits on, looking as wretched as before. The whole thing is a successful farce, which will be played every day, without intermission, for months together.

I recollect a *soi-disant* ex-commercial traveller who used to be wheeled about in a Bath chair, drawn by an attendant. The vehicle was allowed to pass without interference by the police along the footway of a crowded thoroughfare, and might occasionally be seen pulled up close to the entrance of some fashionable shop at an hour when the latter was thronged with customers. The occupant of the chair lolled lazily on his seat, resting himself on his elbow, and holding up a large card on which were inscribed the nature of his profession and the calamity which prevented him from following it. Whether the misfortune were real or feigned it would be impossible to say, but in appearance the man looked quite as healthy as nine-tenths of the people who stopped to give him alms. He was, moreover, respectably dressed, and from the fact of his keeping a Bath chair and an attendant, one might infer that it was not a case of immediate destitution.

I could fill a volume with the interesting stories which I have been told by tramps and beggars who have appealed to me for help in the streets of London. I listen to them whenever I have time. There is the young man who was cruelly turned out of doors at Reigate on the very day of his father's second marriage. There is the journeyman carpenter who has walked all the way from Cardiff in search of a job. There is the woman whose husband had his two legs amputated (above the knees) in the 'Devonport 'Orspital' last week and has come to London for the purpose of finding a cousin (address uncertain) who promised her relief six months ago. There is the girl whose mother, a dressmaker, was confined of twins at Croydon yesterday and who brought up a mantle to a customer in Paddington under the full impression that she would be paid for the work on delivery, but unfortunately the 'lidy' had gone out of town, and consequently how was she to get back to Croydon? There is the boy who slept in the Park last night and has not tasted food ('s'elp' him!) since the day before yesterday, but who, nevertheless, walked away rather sulkily with the bread and cheese which I gave him at my door, leaving an impression on my mind that he intended to chuck it down the nearest area.

The fact is that I have almost entirely abandoned the practice of giving money in the streets, but I promise relief to all who will bring a line of recommendation from even the humblest acquaintance next day. The offer is gratefully accepted. *But somehow they never return!*

I am not conscious that my ordinary expression is one indicative either of extreme benevolence or marked credulity, but it is nevertheless a fact, that in the course of my walks through London I find myself constantly selected as a sort of oracle for the answer of casual inquiries in the streets and parks. Errand boys stop me with the utmost *sang froid* to ask the nearest way to Hyde Park Corner. Shabby children come up and question me as to the time of day. I pull out my watch and inform them, when they at once run off without uttering a word of thanks—ungrateful little wretches! I am chary of the foreigner who wants to know the easiest route to the French Consulate, because I remember him of yore. He sought the same advice of me twenty years ago, and has done so on divers occasions since, always in his mother tongue, generally supplementing his request with a suggestion that, as time is an object and he has forgotten his purse, I might pay his cab fare.

But last winter I had a more novel experience. I was returning home in the dusk of the evening when I was suddenly accosted by a very respectable middle-aged lady, who begged that I would kindly direct her to the nearest station on the Metropolitan line of railway. I told her it was Notting Hill, upon which she at once confided to me that she had taken a return ticket from Tunbridge Wells that morning for the purpose of doing a little shopping in London, but, unfortunately, she had had her pocket picked, and consequently, would be obliged to walk all the way to Charing Cross, unless I were kind enough to lend her ninepence.

For a moment I really was embarrassed. I felt sure that it was a 'do,' but she looked so *very* respectable. Seeing me hesitate she assured me that my little loan would be punctually repaid by postal order. 'I can hardly promise to send it to-night,' she added, 'because the office will be closed. But in the course of to-morrow—if that would be soon enough?'

I begged that she would suit her own convenience on that point, and then I considered for a minute how I could best be even with my lady. At last an inspiration came.

'But,' I said, 'you are evidently a stranger in this part of London?'

'Entirely,' she replied; 'I never was here before!'

'Madam,' I interposed, 'it is growing dark, and I don't like the notion of your walking about at this time of the evening without an escort. Besides, you might not be able to find your way to the station. Allow me to accompany you *and I will take your ticket myself.*' (This proposal was, I think, ingenious.)

'You are really too kind,' she said with rather a forced smile, and we walked away together. Somehow, she did not keep pace with me, but fell a little to the rear. Perhaps she was tired, poor lady! or perhaps she felt shy at walking side by side with a strange gentleman. Anyhow, she lagged behind. But I kept my eye upon her. After we had proceeded for about two or three minutes, I turned round and saw her looking into a shop.

'Here I am!' she exclaimed in a re-assuring tone.

'Well, we are not far from the station now,' said I; and presently we came in sight of it.

Just at that moment a horse fell down in the street and my attention was drawn towards the road for a moment. The station was on the other side of the way, and I turned round once more to assist my fair companion over the crossing. But, strange to say, in that brief interval—so frail and uncertain are the issues of this life—in that brief interval, I say—THE LADY HAD DISAPPEARED! And, what is more, I never saw her again.

A popular professor of *legerdemain*, well known in Piccadilly, used to reserve for the close of his performance a famous trick, described as 'The Vanishing Lady.'

Without attempting to rival his ingenuity, I am reminded by the above-mentioned incident that, having reached the end of a twelfth chapter, it is time for me, too, to make my bow and drop the curtain.

VALETE!

Printed in Great Britain
by Amazon